KIDDERMINSTER AND STOURPORT ELECTRIC TRAMWAYS COMPANY

By

David Voice

Published by Adam Gordon

ALSO BY DAVID VOICE

How to Go Tram and Tramway Modelling, 3 editions
London's Tramways Their History and How to Model Them
What Colour Was That Tram?
Tramway Modelling in 'OO' Gauge
More Tramway Modelling in 'OO' Gauge
The Illustrated History of Kidderminster and Stourport Electric Tramway (with Melvyn Thompson)
The Millennium guide to Trams in the British Isles
The Definitive Guide to Trams in the British Isles
Toy and Model Trams of the World, Volumes 1 & 2 (with Gottfried Kuře)
Next Stop Seaton! 3 editions (with David Jay)
Hospital Tramways and Railways, 2 editions
Freight on Street Tramways in the British Isles
British Tramcar Manufacturers, British Westinghouse and Metropolitan-Vickers
Works Tramcars of the British Isles
The Age of the Horse Tram
Monorails of the World
Tram and Bus Tokens of the British Isles
Battery Trams of the British Isles
Mono-Rail, The History of the industrial monorails made by Road Machines Ltd, Metalair Ltd, and Rail Machines Ltd
Tramway Reflections
Shocking Solutions to a Current Problem
Seaton Tramway – It's Electric
Seaton Tramway – The Valentine's Day Storm
The History of Worcester's Tramways
Last Rides - Funeral Trams Around the World
All Dressed Up and Somewhere to Go, the History of Decorated Tramcars in the British Isles
Slot Machines, The History of Cable-Hauled Street Tramways in the British Isles

A catalogue entry for this book is available from the British Library

ISBN 978-1-910654-13-2
Publication no. 117
Published in 2017 by Adam Gordon, Kintradwell Farmhouse, Brora, Sutherland KW9 6LU
Tel: 01408 622660
Printed by 4Edge Ltd, Hockley, Essex SS5 4AD

KIDDERMINSTER AND STOURPORT ELECTRIC TRAMWAY COMPANY

CONTENTS

FOREWORD

I have been resident in Kidderminster for over forty years and have always had an interest in the history of the town's tramway. Whenever the opportunity arose I collected photographs and information on the tramway. Although a system that was a very small part of the massive British Electric Traction empire, Kidderminster was able to make several claims in tramway history. It was the first tramway to be built on the British mainland that was powered by overhead electrical supply for the whole of its life. It had the first electric tramcars to have windscreens to protect drivers and it was the first to convert trailer cars to electrically powered tramcars.

It had elements of both an urban tramway and an interurban linking two communities. In 1998, to celebrate the centenary of the opening of the tramway, a group of enthusiasts arranged several events to take place. The Mayors of Kidderminster and Stourport were invited to join two groups that walked the route on the anniversary day. One group with the Mayor of Stourport started at the Severn Bridge and walked towards Kidderminster, led by Paul Collins, while the other, with the Mayor of Kidderminster, started at Kidderminster Railway Station and walked towards Stourbridge, led by myself. On the way the groups were shown parts of the town that were eminently recognisable from the tramway days and others that had changed beyond recognition. A look was taken down Tram Street where the depot was located, now the site of an electricity substation. The two groups met each other about half way along, where the Mayors greeted each other and exchanged certificates recognising the event. Then the groups continued on their way. A few days later a celebration dinner was held in "Ye Old Crown Inn", by the Stourport terminus of the tramway. Exhibitions about the tramway were held in Kidderminster and Stourport libraries and finally Melvin Thomson and I wrote and published "The Illustrated History of The Kidderminster and Stourport Tramway", ably assisted by Melvyn's son Andrew.

This photograph was taken soon after the tramway opened with the car in pristine condition. It is equipped with couplings for towing trailers, but these were not needed on the lightly patronised Somerleyton route.

INTRODUCTION

LOCATION

Kidderminster has a long history; it was mentioned in the Domesday Book (1086) as the site of a large manor. It was predominately rural until the 1700s when the local carpet industry began to be developed. The first large carpet factory was opened in 1785 by the Brinton family. The industry expanded, aided by the climatic conditions. The low river valley kept a damp atmosphere that helped keep the hemp and wool in prime condition. By the 1950s there were over 30 carpet factories in the town.

Richard Baxter, a puritan minister, lived in Kidderminster from 1641 to 1660, while its most famous son was Sir Rowland Hill, inventor of the modern postal system. More recently, Robert Plant, of the group 'Led Zeppelin', was raised in the town.

Stourport is a far more modern community. It was created when the Staffordshire and Worcestershire Canal (S&W) was opened in 1768 with a canal basin at its connection with the River Severn. The route of the canal takes it through the centre of Kidderminster. When the S&W Canal was connected to the Birmingham Canal in 1772 it became the main transport for products from the City. Stourport soon became one of the main distribution centres for goods bound for or coming from, the West Midlands. Originally called Stourmouth, then Newport, it acquired its current name in 1771. In addition to the commercial industry, the town soon became famous as a holiday destination for folk from Birmingham and the Black Country.

This aerial view shows some of the many carpet factories that Kidderminster was famous for. The road across the bottom of the photograph is New Road, part of the tram route to Stourport. A tramcar is just visible, partly hidden by the last house in the road. The road to the right of the canal is Castle Road, leading to Dixon Road.

The earliest passenger transport for the majority of people in the area was by foot or horse or carriage for those that could afford it. Farmers taking goods to local markets would often take their employees, but it was not until the early 1800s that transport became more available to workers. There were regular services of horse-drawn coaches linking Kidderminster with other large towns. By the mid-1800s the public horse omnibus was making an impact in many towns, providing a regular service on a defined route to a published timetable. However, it is more likely that a market town like Kidderminster would have a less formal service of brakes and wagonettes. Bulky and heavy goods would travel by barge or narrow boat on canals and rivers.

BACKGROUND

The first street tramway in Britain was opened by George Francis Train in Birkenhead, in 1860, which was the start of a series of horse tramways being opened in towns and cities around the country over the next few decades. They were seen as a route to a pot of gold, however, once the initial frenzy to join was over, it was realised that operating a tramway was more expensive than had been anticipated. The major drain on money was the upkeep of the horses and so other, cheaper, forms of power were sought. Following railway practice, steam became the obvious choice. However, a new and untested power source was emerging, electricity.

The first electrically powered street tramway in the British Isles was the Giant's Causeway Tramway in Northern Ireland. Opening in 1883 it used locally generated hydro-electric power and a third rail supply system. The lack of understanding was such that, on opening day, the VIP visitors were given a tour of the power house and one of the directors went around with a live lead in one hand shaking hands with the visitors giving them an electric shock of several hundred volts!

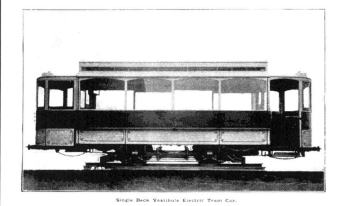

Advertisement for Brush Engineering featuring the Kidderminster motor tramcar.

The first electrically powered tramway on the mainland was opened in Blackpool in 1885, which used the conduit system for current supply.

THE BRITISH ELECTRIC TRACTION COMPANY LIMITED

Emile Oscar Garcke was born in Saxony in 1856. He emigrated to Britain and became a naturalised citizen in 1880. He joined the Brush Electrical Company as its Secretary in 1883 and rose to becomes its Managing Director. He then moved to become Managing Director of the Electric Construction Company, which had a factory in Wolverhampton that, by 1895, covered 23 acres and employed 700 people.

He had a great interest in the development and use of electricity and in 1895 he established the British Electric Traction (Pioneer) Company. The aims of the Company were to arrange the finances of any tramway Company wishing to use electricity as a power source. The Company acquired interests for tramways in Oldham, Hartlepool, Kidderminster and the Potteries. The Company was successful and at the end of its first year it was taken over by another Garcke Company, the British Electric Traction Company Limited (BET), with the aims of developing electric tramways throughout the country through building new lines or converting existing lines.

The success of the original Company enabled Garcke to raise sufficient capital to purchase further existing tramways, initially in the West Midlands. Over the years the Company was to become the largest private owner of tramways in the British Isles. The systems it owned were Airdrie and Coatbridge, Barnsley, Barrow-in-Furness, Birmingham, Birmingham and Midland, Brighton and Shoreham, Cambridge, Cavehill and Whitewell, Devonport and District, Dewsbury Ossett and Soothill Nether, Dudley and Stourbridge, Gateshead, Gravesend, Great Yarmouth, Greenock and Port Glasgow, Hartlepool, Jarrow, Kidderminster and Stourport, Leamington and Warwick, London (Metropolitan Electric and South Metropolitan), Merthyr Tydfil, Mexborough and Swinton, Middleton, Oldham Ashton and Hyde, Peterborough, Poole, the Potteries, Rossendale Valley, Rothsay and Ettrick Bay, Sheerness, South Staffordshire, Southport, South Shields, Swansea, Swansea and Mumbles, Taunton, Tynemouth, Weston-Super-Mare, Wolverhampton District, Worcester, Wrexham and District, and Yorkshire (Woollen District).

The Kidderminster and Stourport Electric Tramways Company published a booklet to advertise the tramcar journey from Kidderminster station to the pleasures of Stourport. The tramway linked with river steamers for trips to Holt, Worcester and Tewkesbury and road trips to Whitley Court, Holt, Ombersley and Hartlebury.

Stourport.

Its Scenery is unrivalled in the Midlands. No Pleasure Resort has proved more enjoyable and interesting. - - - -

How to get there.

Take the Electric Tram just outside the Kidderminster Station. Trams go through 4 miles of delightful scenery into the heart of the country. . . .

EASTER, 1906.—20,000 passengers travelled by Tram to Stourport.

River Trips.

By Finest Steamers on Severn to Holt, Worcester, Tewkesbury, &c. . .

Circular Drives.

entirely through country to Witley Court, Holt, Ombersley and Hartlebury. · ·

Drop Postcard for information to Agents(*see Frontispiece*) for Combined Tram, Steamer or Drive – Cheap Bookings.

Railway Bookings also can be arranged.

CHAPTER 1

PROPOSALS AND CONSTRUCTION

THE FIRST PROPOSALS

Clearly, in the 1890s, the thoughts of Emile Garcke (Managing Director of the Brush Electrical Engineering Company Ltd.) were turning to developing and promoting electrical power for tramways. He and colleagues had been scouting suitable tramway systems to acquire and convert to electrical operation and also towns that were ripe for the introduction of an electric tramway. One such town was Kidderminster, though at the time he did not have a Company able to take any initiative. He seems to have used his contacts to persuade Alfred Dickinson and Company of Birmingham to make the initial moves. In May 1895 the Kidderminster town Council accepted the proposals by the Dickinson Company to apply for a Provisional Order to construct an electric tramway in the town. Alfred Dickinson, owner of the Company, was also the General Manager of South Staffordshire Tramways Company (another tramway destined to be acquired by the British Electric Traction Company).

It was later in May that Emile Garcke established the British Electric Traction (Pioneer) Company with the Earl of Suffolk and Berkshire; John Smith Raworth; Sir Charles Rivers Wilson (Chairman); with himself as Managing Director. The new Company took over the promotion of the Kidderminster tramway and was itself acquired, after just twelve months of existence, by the newly formed British Electric Traction Company Limited (BET). The estimated cost of the whole construction of the Kidderminster tramway was nearly £25,000 (close to £2M at today's values).

The Kidderminster and Stourport Electric Tramway Bill was deposited in Parliament in November 1895, with the necessary plans. It received the Royal Assent on 5th August 1896, allowing the Kidderminster and Stourport Electric Tramway Company to be formed to construct and operate the tramway. The Bill authorised the construction of the tramway in three parts:-

Tramway no. 1, starting in the centre of Vicar Street opposite the centre of the Kidderminster town hall buildings, going along Oxford Street, Bridge Street, New Road, Stourport Road, Foundry Street, Lombard Street, High Street and Bridge Street; Stourport. All single track with eight passing loops.

Tramway no. 2, starting at the intersections of the centre lines of Spirit Lane, Shortheath and Comberton Road (today the junction of Somerleyton Road and Comberton Road), Comberton Hill, Worcester Cross, Oxford Street and terminating at a junction with Tramway no 1 at the junction with Bridge Street. All single track with two passing loops.

Tramway no. 3, starting at the centre of New Road, over the River Stour, to the depot.

The gauge of the tramway was set at 3ft 6in, the common gauge for tramways in the West Midlands. The 4½ miles long line was to be single track with passing loops at the three termini and at intervals along the track. Owing to the narrow nature of some of the roads on the routes the tramway Company was required to widen some roads and bridges. These were the bridge over the River Stour in New Road, Caldwell Bridge in New Road, the bridge over the River Stour in Stourport Road, the bridge over the Staffordshire and Worcestershire Canal in Stourport Road, and widening the Stourport Road in Kidderminster Foreign, Upper Mitton and Lower Mitton.

The track in the conurbations of Kidderminster and Stourport was to be laid along the centre of the roadway, with the road surface built of Clee Hill granite setts, while between the towns, from Foley Park to the start of the built-up area of Stourport, the track was to be at the side of the road, running on its own right of way, with a macadam surface (a road surface made of compressed layers of small broken stones). This part was referred to as a "tramroad", while the road sections were called tramways.

The Consulting Engineers to the tramway were Alfred Dickinson and Company, who also supervised the construction work being undertaken by the building Company, the local firm of George Law of Comberton Hill. This contract led George Law to build a reputation as a renowned contractor for the building of tramways across the West Midlands and further afield.

The depot and, on the right, the power station. The approach was by a bridge over the River Stour . At the front of the depot there was a three way point then two more points, giving five roads within the building. Clearly the tramway Company was anticipating much growth of the system, as the capacity was far more than the initial nine tramcars and trailers.

The Company had chosen a difficult route politically. The line, though very short compared to other tramways, ran over land controlled or owned by four different Authorities. The longest part of the line ran within the control of Kidderminster Corporation; then the other end of the line was within the ambit of the Stourport Urban District Council; the country section of the route ran within the boundary of the Kidderminster Rural District Council, and over some land owned by the Worcestershire County Council. This did not make getting agreements easy, as the different authorities often had different views. So it is not surprising that during the passage of the Bill there were a number of objections that led to requirements to protect the interests of various organisations. Kidderminster Corporation set a limit to the length of the passing loops and required agreement that the tramway would widen roads and bridges where required. The Worcester County Council also insisted that roads in their area had to be widened, while Stourport Urban District Council also had specific requirements in their town. The tramway crossed over the Great Western Railway at three places; over bridges at Kidderminster Station and at Foley Park Halt (the station opened in 1905); and over a level crossing at Stourport Station. The Great Western Railway set conditions for the tramway at these places. There were safety reasons for these requirements, as on the bridges stray currents from the tramway could have interfered with the low voltage signalling on the railway, with unsafe consequences, while the level crossing meant that the railway rails had to be cut to allow the tram rails to be laid. The Great Western Railway required that they installed the crossing with the tramway Company paying for the work.

CONSTRUCTION

Work on building the tramway commenced in July 1897. Mr Law told the local paper that he hoped to have the generating station and depot buildings completed in about two months, ready for the installation of machinery. Work had also started on one of the bridges that required widening. Track laying commenced on the Somerleyton route to the town terminus and thence onto the depot and power station on New Road. This was to enable the tramcars to be delivered by rail to the station and then run on the new track to the depot.

In January 1898 the local paper reported that the newly constructed track and road surface on Comberton Hill was already being damaged by horse-drawn vehicles using a slipper brake when going down-hill. The Corporation introduced By-laws to restrict the weight carried by wagons, with a limit on the total weight of vehicle and goods of 5 ton 15 cwt. The Comberton Hill track was the subject of a query raised by Alderman Herring during a Council meeting. He commented that the rails of the tramway had been laid high and the road surface built up so that there was no longer a step between the road and the pavement. To rectify this, the pavement needed raising. He was told that the pavement would be opened in order to lay the electrical supply cable and at this time the pavement would be raised.

This photograph of tram number 3 was taken soon after the tramway opened. The tiny roof mounted headlight (virtually useless), couplings and lack of life-trays show the "as delivered" state of the tramcars.

A member of the public raised the issue of widening the bridge in Bridge Street, which he felt was too narrow to accommodate the tramway. The authority to build the tramway identified four bridges on the route that required widening, which did not include the Bridge Street bridge. As there was no legal requirement on the tramway Company to undertake such work, they did not respond to the request. The matter was raised in the Council and it was decided not to raise the matter with the County Council (who would be responsible for undertaking the widening), revealing some animosity between the two Councils, the outcome was that the bridge was not widened.

Construction of the lines continued and it was reported in April 1898 that the tramway was nearing completion. The Kidderminster town terminus had been shortened slightly to Oxford Street rather than outside the Town Hall. Most of the track and overhead had been built, the main exception being the level crossing in Stourport. The Great Western Railway had reluctantly agreed, provided they laid the crossing because they wanted to ensure that the tramway electrical return through the rails did not interfere with the currents operating the railway signalling.

The tramway Company approached the Stourport Council to consult over the fares to be charged. The Council members were reluctant to comment as they were rather concerned at the poor quality of track laying within the town. However, they finally concluded that the full fare from one town to the other should be 2d, and that a fare stage should be at Oldington.

Trailer operation only lasted for the first few years of the tramway, so photographs of it in action are rare. This is one of just two known photos of trailers in use.

Tramcars were ordered from the Brush Electrical Engineering Company, a Company with links to the British Electric Traction Company. Three Directors of the BET were also Directors of Brush while Emile Garcke was also Managing Director of Brush. It was natural that BET would order the rolling stock from Brush. For the Kidderminster system nine tramcars were ordered. Six, numbered 1 – 6, were single-deck totally enclosed four-wheel cars, while three were single-deck, cross-bench trailers. These were an unusual design for British tramways of the time and this is discussed in more detail in the chapter on the rolling stock of the tramway. The Brush factory was in Loughborough and the tramcars were delivered to Kidderminster by railway in the first week of April 1898. There is no detail on the arrangements of the transport, but given the railway loading gauge it is probable that they had to be sent with the trucks separate from the body, in the same way as tramcar deliveries to other systems. At Kidderminster station, in the goods yard, the two parts of the tramcar would be assembled. By this time the track had been laid on the Comberton route as far as the depot. So the cars would be moved to the track and taken to the depot. Dynamos had not been fitted in the generator house and so the cars would have been hauled to the depot by a team of horses, who, no doubt, were pleased that most of the journey was downhill.

The depot just before the start of the tramway service. The tramcar fleet has been delivered and most parked in the shelter of the depot.

The first dynamo was fitted during the first week of May and a test of the track was undertaken the following week, using a tramcar hauled by a team of four horses. The first test runs using electrical power (at 550 volts DC) commenced a few days later. A tramcar ran from the depot to the level crossing, which suggests that, while the track for the crossing had been laid (a tramcar hauled by horses had previously travelled to Stourport High Street), it is possible that the overhead was not completed. From the level crossing the tramcar was driven to Somerleyton. Everything must have progressed well as the management invited the Board of Trade Officers to inspect the tramway. This took place on 18th May 1898. It was probably a tense occasion for both the tramway and the inspectors. The Kidderminster tramway was the first overhead electric tramway to be built as new system (as opposed to being converted from a previous type of power). An indication of the importance of the occasion was that the BoT sent two Inspectors, Sir Francis Marindin for the mechanical work and Major Carlow for the electrical equipment. They travelled over the whole line and found it satisfactory.

They approved the tramway and gave permission to open it immediately with the proviso that the line should have speed limits. These were set at 8 mph for travelling on the streets of both towns with a limit of 5 mph along Foundry Street in Stourport, and some of the narrow points in Kidderminster. On the reserved track section (the tramroad) between the towns a higher speed was allowed at 12 mph. Though in practice tramcars did not carry speedometers, so it was up to the driver to estimate the speed. No doubt, if running behind the timetable, the estimation of the speed would be somewhat flexible.

The tramway announced that it would open on Monday 23rd May. It had a couple of weeks previously invited the technical press to a special day to inspect and ride on the tramway. All the eminent magazines, such as The Electrical Engineer; The Engineer; and The Railway World were invited. They were given information and drawings and when they returned to their offices they arranged for the articles to appear at the same time as the opening of the tramway. One piece of information was that the line would open on 23rd May. However, on the appointed day the Company decided it was not ready to provide the public service and postponed the opening to Wednesday 25th May. Instead, the Monday and Tuesday were used for test running. No reason was given for this decision, just that everything was not in order. It is interesting to speculate why the tramway was not ready, after it had passed the exacting Board of Trade inspection. It may well have been to do with the drivers. Clearly there were no electric tramcar drivers available in Kidderminster, so they were recruited from further afield. The drivers were unfamiliar with the geography of the route, particularly as it had long stretches of single track with passing loops not visible from the previous loop. Careful co-ordinated driving was needed to prevent two cars travelling in opposite directions meeting on the single track. In such a case the car nearest a loop would be required to reverse to allow the cars to pass. If they met near the central point between loops, vigorous arguments between drivers was a possibility. In addition, the time needed for the manoeuvre upset the schedule. The two days delay in the official opening may well have been needed to familiarise the drivers with the route, passing places and timetable. The Company used the time to allow the public to have free rides and hence publicise the forthcoming service.

OPENING

The tramway opened officially on the Wednesday 25th May, though without any ceremony, either formal or informal. The first tram of the day for fare paying passengers left the terminus in Oxford Street at 7.00 a.m. with a full load of passengers. During the day the streets of both towns were crowded with onlookers, amazed at such large vehicles moving quietly, with apparently no means of power. Comberton Hill must have appeared particularly impressive with a stationary car easily moving off to go up the hill, while far smaller horse drawn carts were struggling to climb the hill. Such was the demand to take a ride on a tram, they were full of passengers all day. Indeed, there were complaints of folk in Stourport that they could not get on the cars. A full car would arrive at the bridge in Stourport and no one would alight, meaning that the people in the queue at the terminus were unable to board. The service continued until midnight. In its record of the day, the local paper looked forward to the power station of the tramway also being able to supply the town with electricity.

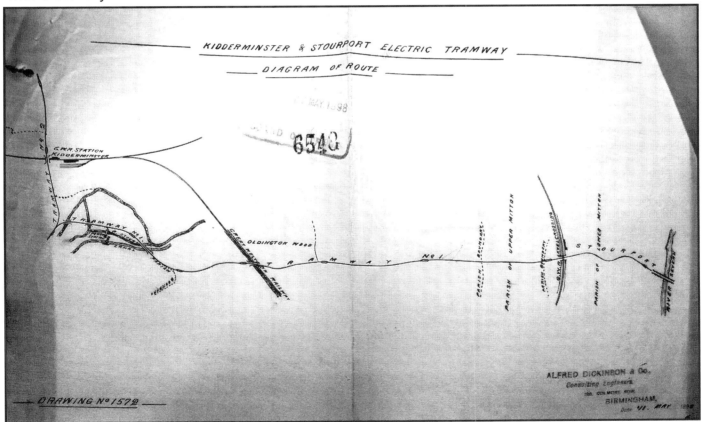

The original diagram of the route prepared by Alfred Dickinson & Company, Consulting Engineers.

It seems that, for the first few weeks, the tramway was experimenting with the service, to determine the best for both itself and the public. The manager kept changing the timetable, meaning that the public could not predict when to catch the tram. It was announced that a timetable would be published by the middle of June. Soon after that announcement the Company wrote to the Council complaining that there were insufficient customers to warrant a more frequent service and they sought permission to lay four new passing loops at Dixon Street; Bonemill Hill; at the bottom of Foundry Street; by the Swan Inn; and also to lengthen the loop at Oxford Street. The matter was referred to the General Purposes Committee.

In August, a letter of complaint appeared in the newspaper stating that the tram drivers were ignoring the signals of members of the pubic in the street who indicated they wished to board the car. It was suggested that plain clothes inspectors should travel the routes to spot errant drivers. There was another letter on 27th August 1898 asking why the tramway had not introduced workmen's car as required under their authorisation. In response the tramway Company said that they would be commencing workmen's cars the following Monday.

There was another complaint the following month from residents in Bridge Street and High Street, Stourport. They sent a Memorial (a formal complaint) to the Stourport Urban District Council complaining about the noise of the tramway, and the facts that it operated after midnight and offered a service on Sundays that was so frequent as to be a nuisance to the residents. They requested that the tramway stopped its service at 10.00 p.m. and reduced the service on Sundays. The Council were sympathetic, but said they had no powers in the matter and the residents should complain to the tramway Company. In September the Council received a letter from the tramway Company stating that the workmen's cars had commenced running. The times of these cars were not published in the newspapers, however, it appears that they ran at 5.30 a.m., 5.35 a.m. and 7.00 a.m. At the same time the Council had agreed and published the Rules and Regulations for the tramway.

The first recorded accident on the tramway occurred on 12th September 1898, just seven weeks after its opening. Mr J. Griffin, described as old and infirm, was standing on the track on Comberton Hill in the path of a descending tramcar. The driver of the tram sounded his bell vigorously, however, Mr Griffin failed to hear or see the tram. By the time the driver realised that Mr Griffin would not move it was too late to bring the car to a halt and it collided with the pedestrian. Mr Griffin was taken home by a nearby policeman and recovered sufficiently the next day to get about.

This is the only other photograph of trailer operation on the tramway, as two tram and trailer sets pass on the loop in Minster Road

In October the BET made an announcement that they were considering building a tramway to link Kidderminster with the Kinver Light Railway at the Stewponey and Foley Arms, via Cookley. The BET were promoting the Kinver Light Railway Order 1898 and had seen this as an opportunity to build a connection to the Kidderminster system that was otherwise isolated from the rest of the BET Black Country tramways. Kidderminster, being promoted in 1895, was bound by the only legislation available at the time, the Tramways Act 1870. With the benefit of hindsight it is clear that things could have been much less onerous for the BET had they waited two years and applied for the tramway under the Light Railway Act 1896, which was much less restrictive than the 1870 Act. The 1896 Act was enacted to encourage the building of rural railways connecting small communities, a good description of the Kidderminster tramway. As events unfolded over the years, the Kidderminster system, like the BET-owned Worcester tramway, remained isolated from any other BET system.

In the same month the tramway Company approached the Council to ask if they could have fixed stopping places. This request shows that, initially, intending passengers could hail the trams at any point on the route. Today it is second nature to only expect public transport to stop for passengers at fixed places. But originally passengers expected that their transport would stop when hailed, like a taxi cab. The Council considered this radical proposal from the Company and agreed, subject to the Company placing notices to inform the public of the new arrangements. The Council agreed to widen the pavement at Sutton Park to enable a queue to be accommodated. The Company also issued its first timetable, printing it in the local paper.

October also saw a letter in the local paper that praised the building of the tramway, but suggested that a waiting room be built at the Oxford Street terminus for the comfort of waiting passengers. It was also suggested that at the termini, and at other places on the route, the Company should place a clock showing the time when the next tramcar was expected. Over time (several years) a waiting room was erected at the Oxford Street terminus, there is no record whether a clock was installed.

The track along the Stourport Road and Minster Road was set to one side on its own right of way. This section was referred to in the Act as a tramroad. Due to the proximity of hedges and walls on the side away from the road, passengers on Kidderminster bound tramcars had to use the driver's platform to enter or leave the car.

Pausing for a photograph on the reserved track of the Minster Road on the way to Stourport. Number 6 is clearly very new, appearing to have just come out of the paint shop.

Later in the month, the Council announced that they had reached agreement with the Kidderminster and District Electric Lighting and Traction Company Limited that the Company would sell electricity to the town in return for paying a rent to the Council. This Company was formed to work the power station attached to the tramway depot, which provided the power for the tramway and would sell excess power to Companies and individuals in the town. The directors of the lighting Company were the same as the tramway Company.

In November the Stourport Council had cause to raise the issue of the bad condition of the road surface at the Bridge Street terminus. It was in need of macadamising and the tramway Company was asked to undertake the necessary work. The Company announced that the demand for the workman's cars had increased and in response they would increase the number of such cars and, in addition, passengers purchasing return tickets would be able to return on any car, at any time on a week day.

During the night of the 22nd November there was a severe snow storm and the next morning the land was covered with several inches of snow. The first car in the morning left the depot just after 5.00 a.m. to go to Stourport. The driver found that the snow had drifted and in places was over two feet deep, stopping him from proceeding. He went back to the depot to get help and a team of men travelled with the car and dug out the snow drifts along the route. The tram eventually reached Stourport after 7.00 a.m. An equally slow return journey meant that it did not reach Kidderminster until around 9.00 a.m.

The BET were keen to use the tramway to promote their tramway enterprises in other towns. They would invite councillors and town officials to all-expenses paid day trips to inspect the operation at Kidderminster. There were two such events in December 1898 when deputations from Carlisle Council and from Newport Corporation visited the tramway on separate days.

The tramway had sought agreement to add five extra passing loops to the system. Three were agreed, one in New Road (by Castle Road); one in Stourport Road by the lane leading to Oldington Farm; and Minster Road by St John's Road. However, the request for a passing loop in Foundry Street was rejected on the grounds that the road was too narrow.

The year 1898 ended with a disagreement between the Stourport Urban District Council and the tramway Company that demonstrated the somewhat fragile relationship between the commercial tramway and the public bodies. The Council raised an issue over the standard of the road surface around the passing loop at the Bridge Road terminus. The Council wanted the Company to repave the road with wooden setts. The Company responded that they were most desirous to comply with reasonable wishes of the Council, but expected the Council to be sympathetic towards the Company's requests, in particular, their request to lay a passing loop in Foundry Street, that the Council had rejected. If the Council were willing to reconsider their decision over the new loop then the Company would be very pleased to comply with the request regarding wooden setts in Bridge Street. The Company added that Stourport was the only public body in the whole of the district which had thrown any obstacles in the way of making the tramway service as convenient as possible. The Council agreed to reconsider the decision on the new loop at their next meeting.

A newly delivered tramcar with a number of nattily dressed men. Who they are has not travelled down the ages, but clearly they feel themselves important (even if others do not). Unfortunately it has not been possible to read the notice in the window of the car, as it may have thrown light on the occasion.

CHAPTER 2

CONSOLIDATION

SETTLING DOWN

The new year of 1899 did not start auspiciously. On the 1st January a tramcar derailed while descending Comberton Hill. A stone had become lodged in the groove of one rail and when the tramcar ran over it, the wheel was lifted out of the groove and the tramcar ran off the rails. The driver was able to halt the car before it hit the pavement, so it stayed uplight. Luckily, there were no passengers in the vehicle, however, the incident caused the road to be closed for an hour while the car was re-railed.

1898 had ended with the Stourport Council agreeing to reconsider their decision to refuse an extra passing loop in their town. The matter was raised at their first meeting in 1899 and it was proposed the Council should grant a new passing loop in Foundry Street, on the condition that the tramway Company address the issues at the Bridge Street terminus. There was discussion about the width of Foundry Street and the disadvantages, or not, of the extra loop. The motion went to a vote and the Councillors rejected the proposal and the tramway Company did not get its loop. Today Lombard and Foundry Streets are still just as narrow. The traffic situation was eased when the town centre by-pass roads of Vale Road, Gilgal and Mitton Street were built, allowing traffic to avoid the narrow roads. Many years after the trams had ceased Foundry Street was made into a cul-de-sac.

Foundry Street was in the news again on 28th January, when it was reported that a trap, in which a Mr Anderson was travelling, was upset and he and his travelling companion were thrown out onto the road. It appeared that a team of workers had been repairing the track and had left a wire across the road. The horse had become entangled with it and was thrown down, pulling the trap with it. The horse was injured and the trap smashed, while the riders were severely shaken.

The Kidderminster Council also discussed the tramway when they had their first meeting of 1899. They had approached the tramway Company to ask if it would help fund the widening of the bridge in New Road. However, the Company had declined to contribute towards the costs of the work. A letter in the local paper for 14th January supported the decision of the Council and again highlighted the narrow nature of the streets. At the following meeting on 4th February it was agreed to instruct the Watch Committee to draft a set of rules and regulations for the conduct of tram drivers, conductors and other persons having charge of the vehicle. The Council wished to have the powers to licence conductors and others connected with the tramway. One Councillor complained that the tramcars were sometimes severely overcrowded. The cars were made to carry 24 persons, but at times it felt like 54. Amid laughter the Mayor commented that it was not compulsory to enter an overcrowded tramcar.

On April 1st the Kidderminster Council announced that they had reached agreement with the electric Company to a scheme to provide electric light in the town, as the Company had recently been authorised to supply electricity to the population and businesses in the town.

Easter in 1899 fell early in May and the holiday proved a very busy one for the tramway. The manager allocated one tramcar for service on the Somerleyton route, no doubt running a shuttle service mainly between the station and the Oxford Street terminus and eight cars (five motor cars and three trailers) worked the Stourport route from Oxford Street to the Bridge Street terminus. They were able to provide a ten-minute service.

At the end of May, on the 29th, the tramway suffered its first fatality when a young boy ran in front of a tramcar and was knocked down. Sidney Alfred Cooper, aged three and a half, was returning home after being at Worcester Cross Sunday School. The tramcar was travelling from the Oxford Street terminus to go up Comberton Hill and it slowed down to stop and pick up passengers

Car number 2 at the Bridge Street terminus in Stourport.

at the Green Street stop. The driver was William Harris, who was employed as a conductor and spare driver. At the inquest, evidence was given that the child had run directly in front of the tramcar, giving the driver no chance of stopping before hitting him. It appeared that Alfred was under the supervision of his brother, aged four, who had gone ahead and had arrived home without realising his brother had been injured. Alfred had been quickly transferred to the infirmary but had subsequently died from his injuries, the wheels of the tram having crushed his legs. At this time there was no requirement for tramcars to have any form of protection for pedestrians falling under the cars. The inquest jury concluded that there had been nothing that the driver could have done to prevent the accident and that he was not to blame. The Coroner was critical of allowing such a young child to be in the supervision of another almost as young. He also commented that the tramway Company should consider fitting some form of guard to the fronts of their vehicle to prevent people from going underneath the car. A fortnight later a letter appeared in the newspaper sending a cutting from the Bradford Daily Telegraph saying that wire guards were fitted to the Bradford tramcars and they had saved the life of a three-year-old boy who had run out in front of a tram. Though injured in the accident, the lad survived and the letter writer suggested the tramway Company should follow the recommendations of the Coroner.

The tramway had a happier occasion on 10th June when the BET hosted a visit from Ilford Urban District Council. Eight members and officers of the Ilford Council were given a tour of the tramway, starting with the power house and those tramcars parked in the depot. They then boarded an open car and set out for a tour of the complete system. On their travels they were shown details of the construction of the line and the system of feeder cables. The visitors expressed pleasure at the smooth working of the system and said that it compared favourably, and in some cases better than, the other tramways they had visited, at Edinburgh, Glasgow, Blackpool and Leeds.

On the 20th June, a horse and cart was being driven along Comberton Road, near Lorne Street, when a tramcar approached from Somerleyton. The horse became restive and despite the driver's efforts it pulled the cart onto the tram track into the path of the tram. The tram driver was unable to avoid a collision and the cart, full of earthenware goods, overturned smashing all its contents with an alarming crash. The tram was delayed several minutes while the road was cleared.

FRAUGHT RELATIONS WITH LOCAL COUNCILS

In June "Bilious Burgess" (then a regular column writer in the Shuttle) commented on what he called "the inglorious war" between the Stourport Urban District Council and the tramway Company over the state of the road at the terminus and the request by the Company to lay an additional passing loop. The Company had retaliated by stopping their trams short and terminating at the Swan, at the top of the High Street. The Council countered by threatening to lift the track along the High Street, because it was not being used, and to charge the cost to the Company. The reporter commented that both parties were ignoring the public interest.

In the same issue he also raised the subject of overcrowding. However, for a newspaper reporter, the writer was extremely honest when commenting about overcrowding on the tramcars. He said "I know nothing of the facts" and then went on to make a number of comments. The gist being that if the tramcar was overcrowded the intending passenger had the choice of waiting for the next car. This was not the case for the last car of the day when everyone would want to board. It was the reporter's view that the inconvenience of too many passengers for a short time was better than seeing passengers being left behind.

Both matters were discussed by the Stourport Council at their next meeting. Regarding terminating at the Swan, the clerk advised the Council that they had the power to lift the track if the tramway Company ceased using it for a period of three months. However, in this instance, the Company did run occasional cars to the bridge and so could claim that the track was being used. On the subject of overcrowding the Council asked if the tramcars were licenced to carry a specific number of passengers, as there was a notice in each car stating that the number that could be carried. It was pointed out that this notice only identified the capacity of the car for seated passengers, it gave no indication of standing passengers. It was agreed that the clerk should be instructed to write to the tramway Company drawing their attention to overcrowding and the lack of use of the line between the Swan and the bridge.

Comberton Hill, the railway station is on the right just beyond the tramcar. This shows a common problem for all street tramways, the wagon descending the hill has deliberately placed its wheels on the rail in order to make a smoother journey, but the wagon is blocking the path of the tramcar.

Car number 2 at the Somerleyton terminus. There are some changes to the tram, there is a new, brighter, headlamp on the dash, the advertising roof boards have been extended to the front of the roof (enabled by the removal of the old headlamp) and an advertisement appears on the side panel (the tramway would contract an advertising agency for a set fee per annum to sell space on their tramcars).

The matter of overcrowding may well have already been addressed by the Company, as they had decided that further tramcars were required to run the system. The first purchase was of two four-wheel open-sided crossbench trailers in June or July 1899 (numbers 10 and 11), with a further two arriving at the end of July (numbers 12 and 13). These were all smaller than the original three trailers. It increased the fleet to six motor cars and seven trailers, while the Board of Trade frowned on motor cars having more than one trailer, so it would seem that one trailer was somewhat redundant. This situation did not last long as in September 1899 the three original trailers were converted to motor cars, giving a fleet of nine motor cars and four trailers. It appears that trailer operation was not a success, as a couple of years later, in 1902, the four trailers had entirely disappeared from the fleet, leaving a real mystery. It has not been possible to uncover where these trailers were made, where they were disposed to and, to compound it all, there are no photographs of any of them.

In July, a notice appeared in the papers to say that the Kidderminster and District Lighting and Traction Company Limited was offering £100,000 shares on the following basis. 5,000 preference shares and 5,000 ordinary shares, of which 3,000 of each had been purchased by the BET. The aim of the new Company was to acquire the shares of the Kidderminster and Stourport Electric Tramway Company and to take over the Electric Lighting Order granted to the Kidderminster Corporation.

The latest episode in the 'war' between the Stourport Council and the tramway was reported to the Council's meeting in August. The clerk reported that a reply had been received from the Company regarding his letter about the abandonment of the line from the Swan to the bridge. In response the Company said that it was impossible, owing to the absence of more passing places, to work an efficient service to the terminus in Bridge Street. They had applied to the Council for extra passing places and until they were able to construct them they must continue to stop at the Swan Hotel. The Company also said that they were well aware of the provisions of their Act and of the Tramways Act and had complied therewith. The Company noted the remarks as to overcrowding and would give instructions accordingly.

The August Bank Holiday saw a record number of day trippers to the area. It was said that the traffic on the tramcars to Stourport was the heaviest yet experienced, with cars running every five minutes, while there were complaints that the service was too slow. The evening return was just as busy and it was gone midnight before the last trippers had boarded transport to go home. Around this time (the exact date is not known) the tramway commenced a parcels delivery operation. This was always a feature of BET-owned tramways and in the case of the Black Country tramways was an extensive operation. Selected shops around Kidderminster and Stourport acted as agents for the parcels service, receiving parcels and placing them on passing tramcars.

The Worcester Cross (a drinking fountain) at the junction of Oxford Street, Worcester Street, Green Street and Comberton Hill.

On Friday 1st September the line saw its second fatality when Alfred Gittins, aged 43, died when he was knocked off a tramcar and trailer while attempting to board it. The accident occurred on Minster Road, by Manor Road. The tramcar was between stops and travelling at around two miles per hour, having just left a stop and preparing to enter the point of a passing loop. Gittins attempted to board the car while it was still moving. Thomas Isaacs was the brakesman situated at the rear of the open sided trailer and he was in a position to see everything that happened. Gittins walked briskly past the trailer and trod onto the step to board the motor car. His head then struck an overhead traction pole and he was knocked off the car, falling between the car and the trailer. Isaacs applied the trailer brake and warned the driver, who applied his brake bringing the tram to a swift halt. By this time Gittins had been dragged under the trailer, though not run over by the wheels. With help of passengers, the tram crew raised the trailer and Gittins was pulled out from underneath and placed on the trailer and taken to the Infirmary. It was determined by the inquest that the traction pole was about 15 inches from the side of the tramcar when Gittins collided with it. This was how the pole had been fitted and it had passed the Board of Trade inspection. The inquest jury reached a verdict of accidental death. No mention was made of the lack of lifeguards, though the matter was obviously of concern throughout the country, as in 1903 the Government introduced laws to require street running tramcars to have a protective guard to prevent people from being dragged along underneath.

The matter of the state of the roads was raised again in the Council. It was agreed that for the Council to repair the roads and recharge the Company might lead to friction and trouble. The clerk suggested that they discuss the matter with the tramway Company and find an agreement by which the Company paid the Council a set sum each year to maintain the road surface. It was felt that this approach would be acceptable to the Company and so the clerk was instructed to seek such an agreement. This was done and in November it was agreed that the Council would maintain the roads adjoining the tramway and the tramway Company would pay £10 per annum for this service.

A visit took place on 6th October 1899 when Councillors and officers of Worcester Council were guests of the BET on a tour to inspect the tramway. The BET had purchased the Worcester horse tramway and wanted agreement from the Worcester Council to convert it to electrical operation. The Council were not particularly inclined to agree and so the BET arranged this visit in order that the Councillors could experience an operating tramway. After a ride on the trams to Stourport and back, a visit was made to the depot and power house. They adjourned to the Lion Hotel for lunch and then visited the Kinver line, then under construction, and rode on the Dudley and Stourbridge lines. Evidently the group was impressed as they agreed to the electrification of the city's horse trams.

During November the local paper reported that of the three extra passing loops that were agreed only one, that in New Road, had been built.

At the end of November a tramcar driven by John Summerfield was descending Comberton Hill and, close to the theatre, it hit a cart in the care of Edward Tolley. Summerfield, the tram driver, had repeatedly rung his bell, but Tolley failed to get his cart completely off the track. The tram struck the cart, badly damaging both vehicles. Summerfield was badly cut from broken glass and splinters of wood, while Tolley fell under his cart which ran over him. Passengers in the tram were very shaken. The accident was referred to in a letter in the local paper suggesting that traffic in the town would be much better if slow moving vehicles would travel as far over on the side of the road as was possible, leaving the centre of the road for faster traffic. It would also minimise the possibility of accidents such as the one in Comberton Hill.

The passing loop at Oldington shows the very rural aspect of the tramway route on the road between the two towns of Kidderminster and Stourport.

In December Mr J. A. Lycett, District Manager of the tramway Company, met separately with the Rural District and Kidderminster Councils detailing the proposed construction of a tramway from the end of Mill Street, Kidderminster, to Bewdley. He suggested that the line was required because there were between 200 and 300 people living in Bewdley who worked in Kidderminster and who currently either walked or went by cart. At this early stage the proposals were that the route would commence from the present terminus in Oxford Street, through Vicar Street, Bull Ring, Mill Street, and Park Butts, up Bewdley Hill, possibly terminating at the Kidderminster side of Bewdley Bridge, or going over the bridge to end in a square on the other side of the river. It was proposed to apply for authority under the new Light Railways Act. When asked if the new route would take parcels and farm produce he said that was his intention. The editorial in the paper supported the proposals to build the line and thus connect the three towns of Bewdley, Kidderminster and Stourbridge. However, he stated that there were difficulties regarding the Bull Ring, which was very narrow. The Kidderminster Council felt that if the line was laid, then it should terminate at the bottom of Mill Street. The track through the Bull Ring should only be used to transfer trams from the depot to and from the route at the start and end of the day. In principle the Councils indicated that they were in favour of the proposal.

There was also a document detailing proposals to add further routes to the system:

(1) From the Bull Ring, along Mill Street to Proud Cross, into Habberley Road to High Habberley then on a private right of way to Habberley Valley and terminating near Habberley House.
(2) From the above route on Habberley Road going through Blakebrook across Bewdley Road along Sutton Road to join the Stourport route at Foley Park.
(3) Starting at a connection near the Somerleyton terminus of the existing route along Chester Road, to Birmingham Road, left along that road to turn right at Radford Road, to Horsefair, terminating at Broadwaters.

In December 1899 the local paper printed a criticism of the tramway Company for running open tramcars for the cheaper, early, workmen's cars during the winter, to the discomfort of the passengers. They felt that once the attention of the tramway Company was drawn to this matter they would be happy to consult with their travelling public.

The dreadful condition of the streets is evident in this photograph. The Opera House marks the beginning of Comberton Hill, while the nearer road is Oxford Street and the Worcester Cross is behind the photographer.

KIDDERMINSTER AND STOURPORT

TRAMWAY ROUTES

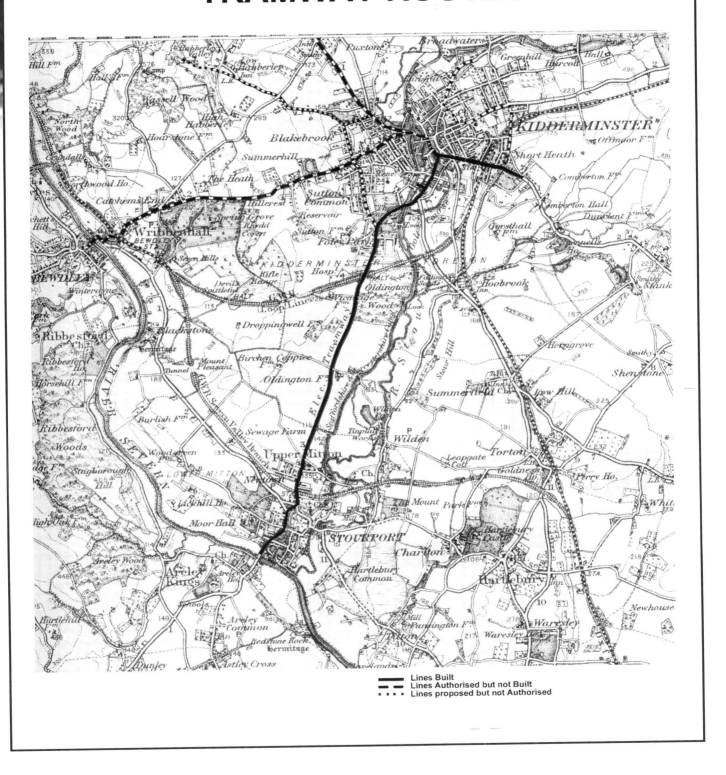

Lines Built
Lines Authorised but not Built
Lines proposed but not Authorised

CHAPTER 3

PROPOSALS FOR EXPANSION

AMBITIONS

While the start of the 21st century was celebrated on 1st January 2000, one hundred years previously the new 20th century was not celebrated at the start of 1900, but a year later on 1st January 1901. It all depends on how you count (or for commercial organisations how long they are prepared to wait).

In January 1900 the proposal to build a tramway to Bewdley was raised again in Kidderminster when Mr Lycett appeared before the town Council. During the meeting Mr Lycett made it clear that the tramway Company were apprehensive that the proposed line would not be a financial success. If any of the three Councils objected to the line the Company would not continue with the scheme. It appeared that this was a ploy to lay the ground to later seek financial support from the Councils, particularly at Fountain Hill, where the road was very narrow and would require rock to be moved to widen it.

At its meeting in January 1900 the Watch Committee granted licences to the tramway for its tramcars and revealed some interesting information. The six original enclosed motor cars were licenced to seat 24 passengers, the three open motor cars (originally trailers) could seat 36 passengers, two of the new trailers purchased in 1900 seated 24 passengers while the final two trailers seated 16 passengers. This confirms that the four 1900 trailers were significantly smaller trailers than the original three and, indeed, two of the new ones were even smaller.

In February, Mr Lycett sent the Kidderminster Shuttle a copy of a booklet published by the BET titled "Tramways and the Housing of the Working Classes". Generally, the working classes needed to live within walking distance of their workplace. This led to overcrowded living conditions within unhygienic areas and close to unhealthy factories. In the United States and Canada, electric tramways had provided affordable public transport allowing workers to live in cleaner areas further away from factories to the benefit of all. The booklet regretted that this was not the case in Britain, where Councils sought financial advantage from any application by a Company to build a tramway. However, it also recognised that tramway Companies paid too much regard to the dividends to their shareholders than the service to the community. The booklet also criticised the Tramways Act for enabling public bodies to purchase operating tramways at their scrap value.

At the meeting of the Bewdley Council the tramway Company asked for permission to run their tramcars over Bewdley bridge, terminating in the square in Load Street. The Council discussed the issue and finally, by a majority, agreed that the Council would not object to trams running over the bridge.

The Kidderminster and Stourport Electric Lighting and Traction Company held its second General Meeting on 25th April 1900 in London, with Mr J. R. Raworth in the Chair. The profit for the tramway was £2,108 14s 10d. He reported that the Council had agreed that the Company take over its electric-lighting Order. It was expected that electric lighting would be operational later in the year. What was not revealed was that the B.E.T. had an agreement with the tramways Company that they (the BET) would provide the services to the Company of a Company Secretary (and support), Traffic Superintendent, Permanent Way Engineer and a Power Engineer, for such time as was necessary to carry out their duties, all for the sum of £175. At this time the tramway Company was employing 47 permanent staff, comprising 20 drivers and conductors, 9 car washers and labourers, 6 carpenters, enginemen and firemen, 3 clerks, 2 linesmen, 1 inspector and 6 others. The arrangements for staffing the tram and trailer sets was to use four staff. The motor car would have a driver and a conductor, while the trailer would have a conductor and a brakeman, the latter stayed on the rear platform and would apply the handbrakes on the trailer when halting at stops and in emergencies. The conductor on the motor car was also responsible for attending

The terminus at Oxford Street, with a car standing on the Stourport track, the normal stopping point for that route. The Somerleyton route terminated at the Green Man and Still, the second building on the right, with the large wall lantern.

OXFORD STREET, KIDDERMINSTER

to the overhead trolley. On most tramways the conductor would watch the trolley wheel through overhead frogs, ready to catch the rope if it de-wired, and turn the trolley pole around when the car reversed. On the Kidderminster system there was only one overhead frog. The whole route (apart from a small section at the town terminus of the Comberton route) was fitted with double overhead wire and so passing cars were already on separate wires. The place where frogs may have been expected was at the Oxford Street terminus where the Stourport and Comberton routes met. However, there were three overhead wires, two for the Stourport route and one for the Comberton Hill route. On the latter the double wire continued along Comberton Hill and along most of Oxford Street. Near the junction of the two routes, the two wires of the Somerleyton route overhead joined at a self-directing frog for the single wire leading to the terminus, During bank holidays and summer weekends large crowds would arrive at Kidderminster station and board trams for Stourport. The Company would place additional conductors at the Comberton Hill stop who would sell tickets to the waiting passengers, so easing the task of the conductors on the tramcars. They would travel to Stourport to do the same at the bridge terminus. In the evening the tramcars would soon become filled, so some day trippers would walk up the High Street, board an incoming tram and pay the fare to the terminus and then stay on the tram for the return trip to Kidderminster, thus jumping the queues.

In May, Dr Martin had cause to complain to the tramway Company when he received unjustifiable treatment from conductor Isaacs when travelling to Stourport. The Company instructed the conductor to write a letter of apology to the Doctor. Conductor Isaacs did so and Dr Martin said he would not take any further action in the matter.

A ROUTE TO BEWDLEY?

On 26th May 1900 the tramway Company wrote to the Light Railway Commissioners to inform them that the Company was making an application for an Order under the Light Railways Act, 1896, to build light railways in the boroughs of Kidderminster and Bewdley and the parish of Kidderminster Foreign. The Company proposed the following railway lines:

A Railway (No. 1) 6 furlongs 0.20 chains in length commencing in Oxford Street, Kidderminster, by a junction with the existing tramways authorized by the Kidderminster and Stourport Electric Tramway Act 1896, at their termination; passing thence along Oxford-street, Vicar-street, Bull Ring, crossing the bridge over the river Stour, thence along Mill-street, Park Butts, and Bewdley-street, and terminating in the latter street near the Green at a point 35 yards or thereabouts south -west of the junction of Bewdley-street with Brook-street.

A Railway (No. 2) 2 miles 3 furlongs 1.20 chains in length commencing in Bewdley-street, Kidderminster, by a junction with Railway No. 1 at its termination, passing thence along Bewdley-street and the main road from Kidderminster to Bewdley and terminating in the latter road at Wribbenhall, near the bridge carrying the roadway over the River Severn, at a point 46 yards or thereabouts north-west of the Bridge Inn.

A Railway (No. 3) 9.80 chains in length, commencing by a junction with Railway No. 2 at its termination, passing thence over the River Severn, into and along Load-street, Bewdley, and terminating in that street at a point opposite the George Hotel.

A Railway (No. 4) 2 furlongs 7.45 chains in length, commencing in Mill-street, Kidderminster, by a junction with Railway No. 1 at a point 10 yards or thereabouts east of the junction of Mill-street with Park Butts, passing thence along Mill-street to and terminating at Proud Cross at a point 5 yards or thereabouts south-east of the junction of Puxton-lane with Mill-street.

Railway (No. 4A) 1.40 chains in length, commencing in Mill-street, Kidderminster, by a junction with Railway No. 4 at a point 12 yards or thereabouts north-west of the western corner of the junction of Mill-street with Park Butts, passing into and terminating by a junction with Railway No. 1 at a point 10 yards or thereabouts south-east of the same corner.

A Railway (No. 5) 6 furlongs 3.00 chains in length, commencing at Proud Cross, Kidderminster, by a junction with Railway No. 4 at its termination, passing thence along Franche-road into and terminating in Bridgenorth-road by the Three Crowns and Sugar Loaf Public-house at a point 17 yards or thereabouts north-west of the junction of the cross roads by the said public-house.

The application for the new tram routes was discussed by the Kidderminster Council on 20th June 1900. The Council agreed to support the application to construct the tramway between the two towns, subject to certain portions of the road being widened. The proposed tramway was to run within the boundary of the Rural District. The Rural District discussed the detailed proposal during their July meeting. In regard to the narrow road through the Bull Ring (the road was just 16ft 7in wide at this point), it was a condition set by the Kidderminster Council that the Company could only use that part of the line during the hours of 6am to 8am and 8pm to 12 midnight to transfer tramcars to and from the depot, without carrying any goods or passengers. The Council voted to support the proposed tramway on the condition that the roads would be widened to 30 feet at the expense of the Company. In response the Company's representative said that this would be an enormous expense for the Company and would make the scheme financially unattractive. At their next meeting the Bewdley Council again discussed the question of whether the tramway should be allowed to cross the bridge, with Council members being very divided about the issue.

Also in June a local bus and brake proprietor, Mrs Sarah Hodge, sued the tramway Company for £5 damages after a collision on Comberton Hill between one of her horse buses and a tramcar the previous 31st March. She claimed that the tramcar was speeding and hit the bus. The tram driver said that he was travelling within the speed limit. The judge concluded that the tram driver had not been able to stop the car as quickly as it ought to have been and awarded Mrs Hodge the full amount she claimed.

The Light Railway Commissioners held an inquiry at the town hall, Kidderminster on 17th October. During the inquiry it transpired that the Mayor of Kidderminster lived in Franche and he supported the proposals for both lines. Most of the discussion focussed on the narrow roads leading past the Black Boy Hotel and over Bewdley bridge. After the enquiry the commissioners were taken along the proposed routes in order to examine the difficulties first hand. The 10th November edition of the local paper carried the conclusions of the inquiry. The commissioners said they would submit the proposal to the Board of Trade to sanction the whole of the routes applied for. They agreed to the tramway being laid in the narrow roads, subject to any regulations required by the Board of Trade. The Councils were disappointed that the Commissioners had not supported their views that the Company should be required to widen the narrow roads as a condition of the construction of the lines. The councillor who had a shop along the narrow part of the Bull Ring objected to any suggestion that his shop should be demolished in order to widen the road.

December 1900 saw another fatality on the tramway. In the early evening of 15th, Alfred George Jeffrey boarded the tram in Kidderminster and travelled to the corner of Sutton Road where he alighted. He then appeared to walk towards Stourport. It was early evening and the roads were dark and evidence was given that Jeffries had been drinking that evening and was not sober. A short while later, a following tram was being driven by Frank Weaver up Bonemill Hill, when Jeffrey was sighted directly in front of the car. He was staggering around and though the driver applied an emergency stop the car hit Jeffrey. The headlamp was smashed in the impact and Jeffrey fell under the car. The driver assessed the car as going ten to twelve miles per hour when he applied the brakes. The driver then said that the guard on the tram pushed the man forward. There was no further description of the guard given during the inquest. Looking at photographs, all the tramcars fitted with couplings did not have life-guards or life-trays. It is more than likely that what the driver was describing was a pilot board, a plank fixed across the ends of the truck. Its purpose was to prevent objects from being run over by the wheels. However, unlike the life-tray it pushed the object along, it did not scoop them up. Jeffrey was carried aboard the tramcar and taken to the infirmary, where he died of his injuries two days later. The jury recorded a verdict of accidental death.

Motorised ex-trailer number 9 in Oxford Street is travelling up the Comberton route. The single overhead of the terminus becomes dual wired at the nearest traction pole.

By the look of the trees it looks like spring time on Comberton Hill with tramcar number 6 on its way to town. This photograph was taken in the early days of the system, as the car still has its coupling for trailer operation.

The start of 1901 saw the country in mourning after the death on 22nd January of Queen Victoria at Osborne House on the Isle of Wight. The newspapers carried black edges to all their columns, irrespective of content (including the advertisements). The funeral took place on 2nd February.

Later in February the supply of electricity to Kidderminster began. The town hall and library were the first municipal buildings to be equipped. The comment from the newspaper was some disappointment as the lampposts did not seem as large or impressive as the previous gas apparatus. Unsurprisingly they also complained that the Company had been digging up the highway, yet again and that compared to the price of gas, electricity was far more expensive.

In March both Kidderminster and Bewdley Councils were still raising objections to the proposed tramway, though what they said was just a restatement of previous opposition. In the meantime, Stourport Council was pondering electric lighting. The issue under debate was whether the Council should apply for a Provisional Order, costing £150, that would empower them to supply electric current to the town, or to leave it to a private Company to do so. It was agreed that the Council should apply for the Order as it would give them more authority in the matter. They were not obliged to supply electricity, but could agree for a Company to do so, as Kidderminster Council had done. If they took this path they would be in a stronger position to negotiate with a private Company and could reclaim their costs as part of the agreement.

The third Ordinary Meeting of the Kidderminster and District Electric Lighting and Traction Company Limited was held on 17th May 1901 in London with Mr J. S. Raworth in the chair. The Kidderminster and Stourporrt Electric Tramway Company (wholly owned by the lighting and traction Company) generated a profit of £2,201. Orders for electricity were good and arrangements were in hand to install new generating capacity to meet the demands. It was hoped that the tramway extension to Bewdley would be begun during the rest of the year.

May also saw additions to the tramcar fleet. Three double-deck, open-top, tramcars were delivered. This was a new venture for the tramway as, up until this delivery, all the tramcars had been single deck. One explanation was that as summer was coming passengers would have the opportunity of enjoying the weather on the open top deck (conveniently forgetting that winter was just a few months away). It was implied that these were new cars, but in fact they were part of a large order by the B.E.T. And two of them (numbers 19 and 25) were second-hand from the Dudley and Stourbridge tramway. The third (number 10, replacing the old number 10) came from the reserved stock held by the B.E.T. They were all originally single deck cars delivered in 1900, but were rebuilt in 1901, for Kidderminster, as double deck cars, with reversed stairs. As rebuilt they had seating for 26 in the lower saloon and 25 on the upper deck and were fitted with couplings for hauling trailers, though by this time there were only four trailers for the 13 motor cars.

In 1901 the system acquired its first double-deck tramcars with numbers 10, 19 and 25 coming second-hand from Dudley and Stourbridge tramways and the BET reserve stock. Here number 19 stands outside Brinton Park.

The 1901 August Bank Holiday Monday was very busy with two cars operating the Somerleyton route and the remaining fleet working on the Stourport route. Indeed, the service had changed earlier in the year and the through service from Somerleyton to Stourport was split into two separate routes. The Bank Holiday Tuesday was disappointing with fewer people travelling than the previous year. This was due to the Great Western Railway running two large excursion trains directly to Stourport, rather than Kidderminster

In September the B.E.T. wrote to the Council to say that as soon as they were legally empowered to construct the tramway between Kidderminster and Bewdley no time would be lost in carrying out the work. Later in the month the authority for the tramway arrived from the Board of Trade. In the same month the electric Company had installed lighting in the Post Office and the tramway Company had erected an electric light at the terminus in Oxford Street.

On 8th October 1901 the Board of Trade authorised the Kidderminster and Bewdley Light Railways Order 1901, enabling the Company to build the tramway. However, there was a sting in the tail. The Councils had got their way and the section of track through the Bull Ring was only to be used for the transfer of tramcars not carrying passengers early morning and late evening. At any other time the tramcars were banned from using that portion of track.

The following month the tramway Company announced that the fare for the journey from Oxford Street to the entrance of the Waterworks in Green Street (by New Street) would be reduced to one penny.

In November a new turbine engine was installed in the power station. Steam from the boilers drove the turbine blades to produce power. It was one of the most up to date steam plants in the country. Mr A. J. L. Plunket, Power Superintendent in Kidderminster, was appointed as Superintendent at the Merthyr and District Electric Traction and Lighting Company Limited (another subsidiary of the B.E.T.).

Another of the three double-deck tramcars, number 10($_2$), came from the BET reserve stock and, like the other two, was converted from a single-deck car.

The newspaper commented on the length of time that the Bewdley branch was taking. It was first mooted by the tramway Company in December 1899, some two years previously, and yet no move had been made to lay any rails. A spokesman for the tramway Company explained that getting Parliamentary approval was a lengthy process and now that approval had been granted they expected that work on the line would start early in the New Year. However, the report did mention that some people thought that the only reason the tramway Company sought authority to build the line, was not because they wanted to add it to their network, but to prevent any other Company from applying for authority to build the line.

In December, the tramway Company announced that they would not be operating a service on Christmas Day, while on the following three days the tram service would not start until 7.45am. The workman's cars would not run. At the start of January, they published the record of the previous year's work. Over the twelve months the tramway carried 719,918 passengers had an income of £6,282 17s 8d. and ran 183,102½ miles.

Stourport High Street with car number 10 leaving the town for Kidderminster. It is passing the Swan Hotel. The tramcar is a striking contrast to the dapper driver of the horse-drawn carriage.

The New Year saw an event that was more like a scene out of a comedy film than a potentially dangerous accident. Mr F. Nicholls was driving his car along Bridge Street and attempted to turn left into New Road. Then he found that the wheels of his car had become trapped in the groove of the tram rails. When they suddenly became free the car swerved and hit a lamppost, bending the post and badly damaging the front of his car. Fortunately, the driver was not injured.

An announcement in the 15th March 1902 newspaper gives an insight into the Bank Holiday arrangements used by the tramway. For Good Friday at Easter the tramway announced that they would be running a Sunday timetable, then on the Easter Monday and Tuesday the workmen's cars were suspended and the service started at 7.40 a.m. with twenty minutes between cars until 10.10 a.m. when it became a ten-minute service, finishing with the 11.30 p.m. from Bewdley. The Comberton Hill route would get its normal ten-minute service. There was also a notice that during the summer the Stourport route would terminate at the Swan Hotel in order to provide a ten-minute service.

Comberton Road looking towards the Somerleyton terminus where tram number 2 stands.

On the 19th April there was a collision on Comberton Hill when George Waite was driving a wagon fully loaded with bags of grain. Some of the bags overhung the wagon and a passing tramcar hit the bags on the wagon and dislodged them, breaking the windows on the tram. Luckily a bag fell off the front of the wagon and jammed under a wheel, preventing the horse from bolting. The paper reported that no blame was attached to the wagoner, which infers that it was the tram driver who was to blame.

Around March/April 1902 the four trailers disappeared from the official returns. The speculation was that the motor cars were low powered and hauling trailers slowed them down. This would be most felt in the rush hours when the heavily laden trailer sets would impede the other trams.

In May 1902, the Kidderminster and District Electric Lighting and Traction Company held its fourth Annual General Meeting in London. The Chairman, Mr William L. Magden, said that he had sad news as their colleague, Mr Sugrue, had recently died. He summarised the holdings of the Company as the Kidderminster and Stourport Electric Tramway Company and powers under the Electric Lightings Acts to supply electricity for lighting and other purposes to the town of Kidderminster. Powers had been acquired to extend the tramway from the Kidderminster terminus to the town of Bewdley. The tramway had an income of £6,303 and made a profit of £2,863 7s 6d. It carried 806,979 passengers for the year. On the electricity supply side the Company had started to sell electricity to the public during the last four months of 1900. A total of £182 had been sold. In 1901 the sales amounted to £2,747, this despite strong competition from the gas Company. He announced a dividend payment for ordinary shares of 2%. Finally retiring directors were re-elected.

DELAYS ON BEGINNING BUILDING THE BEWDLEY EXTENSION

In May the Kidderminster Council raised the issue of the Bewdley extension. It was stated that there was a rumour that the tramway Company Directors had decided to abandon the scheme. The local paper contacted the Company to ask if this was true and, again, the official statement was that there was no foundation to such rumours. Indeed, the Company said they had recently agreed to the general estimates for the work and had instructed that detailed estimates and plans be prepared. It was not intended to commence laying the tramway until the autumn. The tramway was to be completed and running in the early part of 1903.

At the end of May, the paper copied an article previously published in the Wolverhampton Chronicle that extolled Stourport as a holiday destination. Readers were advised to take the railway to Kidderminster Station and then board one of the comfortable trams to ride to Stourport. There were opportunities to take a boat on the river to Holt or Ombersley, or to walk across the bridge and along pretty country lanes.

There was a rather strange announcement in the paper for 28th June 1902 when it was reported that the tramway Company had abolished fixed stopping places and would pick-up and set-down passengers on request. No explanation was given for this change.

A meeting of residents was held on 11th June in the Land Oak Inn to support a request to the tramway Company to ask them to build an extension to the tramway along Chester Road (now called Chester Road North). A deputation of five was selected (including two councillors) to meet with the directors of the tramway. The meeting took place on 19th July and the tramway directors said it would be raised at the next director's meeting. However, it was felt that Kidderminster could do more to help the directors than they had done up to the present. The petition with 186 signatures was considered very influential. Another meeting was held on the 9th December at which it was stated that the Committee and the tramway Company were in discussions. The extension of the line would require an injection of capital and that this had to come from local capitalists. Five gentlemen had been found who were willing to invest £1,100 between them. The Company had responded by saying that they needed to sell £8,000 worth of shares.

The subject of the lack of progress of action on the Bewdley extension was again raised in the local newspaper. It reported uneasiness at the absence of any building, despite the encouragement of leading inhabitants.

The Coronation of King Edward VII took place on 9th August 1902, having been postponed from the original date of 25th June at the last minute due to the King's illness. The King told the country that it was his wish that the celebrations that had been planned for the Coronation Day should go ahead. The tramway Company had decorated tramcar number 3 to celebrate the occasion. Unfortunately, the only record of the decorated car is a photograph of it at the Green Man and Still Hotel. No record exists, but it seems very likely that the tramcar ran in its decorated condition from the original date to the revised celebrations.

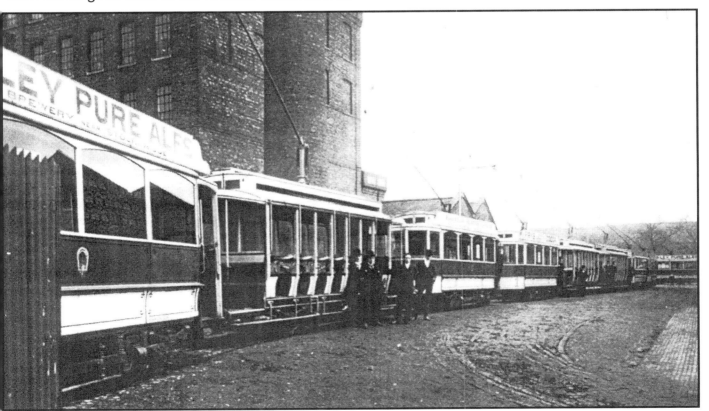

The fleet of the power cars with the first trailers (now motorised) outside the depot.

Tram number 11 in Stourport with the High Street decorated for Empire Day.

Thomas Combs, a carter from Astley, was driving his horse and cart along the Stourport Road. A tramcar was being driven from Stourbridge to Kidderminster and came across Mr Combs when nearing Oldington. It was clear he was drunk, as the cart was on the wrong side of the road. The tramcar driver stopped his car to avoid a collision. The cart moved off the tram line, but collided with another vehicle. Mr Combs was fined 10s with costs.

The Bewdley Council raised the issue of the tramway line to its town. At a meeting on 29th November, Councillors again discussed the matter. It was noted that nearly two years had passed since the Company had been granted authority to build the line. Despite all the loyal assistance the Council had given to the Company no progress had been made on constructing the line. The Town Clerk had said he had written to Mr Lycett and had received an apology stating that the Company had intended starting building the line by now, but other commitments had interfered with the work. They would definitely start construction early next spring. This was also raised at Kidderminster Council's December meeting and mention was made of the communication the Company had given to the Bewdley Council. However, Kidderminster had other problems on its mind over the chaotic state of the pavements after the Company had laid electric cables

For a Christmas treat Mr John Brinton treated 25 of the tramway employees to a meal at the Coffee Tavern. Mr Brinton is of the Brinton family, owners of the Brintons Limited carpet works. The previous year he had given dinner to the employees at the railway station. Mr Brinton was unable to be present and his place was taken by Mr H. F. Pearse of Brintons Limited who read out a letter from Mr Brinton thanking the employees of the tramway for all the work they had done for the community in ensuring there the public transport ran from early in the morning until late at night, whatever the weather. The meal and speeches were concluded with a musical evening.

The tramway Company had another attempt to persuade the Council to allow them to run tramcars through the Bull Ring as part of the Bewdley line. Once again the Council considered the road too narrow to allow tramcars to run on a regular basis. Both the Council and the Company wanted the road widened, but neither wanted to pay the cost. It was suggested that both should contribute to the costs of widening the road, but this fell on stony ground. It was not helped by one Councillor saying that his premises in the Bull Ring would be demolished if the road was widened. The decision reached was to refer the matter to the General Purposes Committee.

The Annual General Meeting of the Kidderminster and Stourport Electric Tramways Company was held in London in March 1903. It was announced that the overall income was £6,494 (including £100 of advertising revenue) that gave a profit of £2,357. The number of passengers carried in the year was 843,111

In April, William Dowell, a linesman for the tramway, was working on a horse-drawn tower wagon in Bridge Street, when the wire he was working on snapped. It hit Dowell, knocking him off the top of the tower and he landed on the roof of a shoeing forge. A policeman and a passing workman managed to get him off the roof and he was taken to the infirmary where he was examined and found not to have any broken bones, but he was badly bruised and severely shaken.

At their meeting in May the Kidderminster Councillors asked the Town Clerk if he had heard anything further from the tramway Company regarding the Bewdley extension. The clerk said that although Mr Lycett from the tramway had promised that work on the line would start, it appeared that they were saving their money in order to purchase the Birmingham tramways. Councillor Baker asked how long it had been since the Company had obtained the Act to build the tramway. The answer was about three years. Some Councillors expressed the opinion that the Company had suspended all operations on the extension and seem to be playing with the Council and was making fools of the Councillors. They have just stopped anyone else from applying for authority. A Councillor suggested that someone might like to instigate a motor car service between Kidderminster and Bewdley, as there was nothing to stop that. Another Councillor suggested that the lack of progress may be connected with the Council's refusal to allow trams to operate a public service through the Bull Ring. Reference was made to Gloucester where they planned to run electric cars without rails (trolleybuses) at a far less cost than building a tramway. The debate ended with no conclusion.

The weather for the Spring Bank Holiday was fine, better than the previous year and the numbers of passengers reflected this with 16,465 passengers travelling compared with the previous year of 11,852.

In the June meeting of the Kidderminster Council the Bewdley extension was raised again. Mr Lycettt had written to the Council asking if they would reconsider their refusal to allow the tramway to operate a public service through the Bull Ring. The Company wished to run one car each way per hour through the Bull Ring. Mr Lycett suggested that the Company should meet with the Council. Colonel Talbot proposed the motion that the request be granted. It was seconded by Mr Taylor. It was suggested that rather than reach a decision at this meeting, the issue should be referred to the General Purposes Committee. Colonel Talbot agreed and the proposition was modified to suit. Mr Grosvenor objected and put his own proposal that the Council do not change their original decision on the matter and reject the tramway Company's request. This was put to the vote and passed 13 votes to 3. At the following meeting, in July, the Councillors were read a letter from Mr Lycett in which he said that the Company regretted that the Council could not see their way to agree to the Company run a tram service through the Bull Ring. He hoped that the Council would take steps to widen the Bull Ring. The Council were prepared to move on the matter, provided the Company would bear a fair proportion of the cost. At an informal meeting with Mr Lycett he suggested that the Council formulate such a scheme for consideration.

On Saturday 25th July an evening tramcar travelling from Stourport to Kidderminster came across a man lying across the track. The driver made an emergency stop but his life guard hit the man and pushed him a short distance along the track. The man was unconscious and was taken to the Infirmary. He recovered consciousness the next day. Apparently he had crossed the track with the intention of catching the tram, when his foot caught in the groove of the near rail, tripping him up. On falling he struck his head and lost consciousness and was hit by the tramcar.

In July an article by Chalmers Roberts entitled "A Trip on a Tram" appeared in The World's Work that is of interest to us. It describes a journey he made from Wolverhampton to Stourport by tramcar. Having reached Kinver he needed to walk for two hours to cover the five miles to Kidderminster. He extoled the delights of the beautiful views of the countryside between Kidderminster and Stourport, following the course of the River Stour.

There was a head-on crash on 16th August 1903 when two tramcars met on a section of the single track. The incident started when a tramcar from Stourport waited at the passing loop by the railway bridge at Foley Park Halt (the station actually did not open until 1905) where it was timed to pass the car from Kidderminster. The driver, Heliwell, waited five minutes with no sign of the other car. He thought he would have time to reach the Sutton Road loop. The approach to the loop was on a curve with overhanging trees obscuring the view along the road. No doubt the car from Kidderminster was driving rapidly to make up time. Both drivers saw the other's car and applied an emergency brake, slowing the cars, but not sufficiently to prevent them colliding. The dash of one car was broken by the impact and Helliwell had slight knee and hand injuries. Thankfully none of the passengers were hurt, though they were alarmed and shaken. Surprisingly the paper reported that since the line had opened there had been no serious accidents which bore testimony to the care and attention exercised by the drivers. A statement that overlooked the three fatalities the system had previously experienced.

A public meeting was held on 18th September to discuss the progress (or lack of) on the Bewdley route. The meeting elected Colonel Talbot to chair the meeting. He said that the point of the meeting was to determine if the tramway extension should halt at the end of Mill Street or should provide a service between Bewdley and the railway station at Comberton Hill. He understood that, unless the tramway Company had permission to run a service through the Bull Ring, they would not construct the line. The Council were criticised by some members of the public for having missed the opportunity of building the tramway themselves and so benefiting residents from the profits made. It was inferred that the Council was anti the tramway Company because they were jealous of the Company. Mr S. Whitcomb said that he had been against the tramcars until he visited Plymouth which had an extensive tramway system some of which travelled through very narrow roads. It was added that the Bull Ring had caused difficulties for many years and that there had been talk of widening it for 20 to 25 years. Now the Council were trying to throw the expense onto the tramway Company. The meeting unanimously resolved to place pressure on the members of the town Council to come to terms with the tramway Company and grant them powers to run tramcars in the Bull Ring. This was followed in the same issue by a letter in the paper criticising the meeting and stating it had no mandate to speak on behalf of residents. The writer supported the stance of the Council.

Car number 8 outside the Roebuck Hotel, Oxford Street.

Below: Car number 4 (rebuilt to double-deck) with the second number 10, delivered to Kidderminster as a double-deck car, but originally built as single-deck.

In October 1903 the new Opera House was opened on Comberton Hill, usefully on the tram route. In the same month the Council had received a letter from the Board of Trade indicating that the tramway Company had applied for an extension of time to complete the Bewdley line (construction of which had not yet been started). At the same time the Council had received a letter from a public meeting asking for the Council to approve a tramway service along the Bull Ring. The matter was at a delicate stage and the Council had asked a Committee to examine the request. The Council decided that it would not be appropriate to discuss the matter, they would rather wait until the Committee had undertaken its examination and made recommendations.

Above: A converted trailer car on Stourport High Street, heading to the bridge.

CHAPTER 4

THE BEWDLEY DEBATE CONTINUES

IS IT ON OR OFF?

The start of 1904 brought a possible solution to the provision of public transport between Kidderminster and Bewdley. The Kidderminster Motor and Cycle Company Ltd had recently been established with a capital of £5,000 with the aim of providing an omnibus service between the two towns. The backers to the Company were all businessmen from one or other of the towns. The service was expected to start in February with an hourly frequency, or half hourly at busy times. Initially the route would have a terminus at the Kidderminster town centre, but it was possible that the route could start at the railway station on Comberton Hill.

In Stourport a tramcar was derailed in Foundry Street at 9 a.m. on 17th February. It was climbing the hill while the road was being repaired. It is probable that stones got into the groove in the rail, causing a wheel to be lifted out, derailing the car. Luckily the car ran clear of the track enabling other tramcars to pass by. The maintenance crew were able to re-rail the vehicle by 11 a.m.

In April the Kidderminster Council received a letter from the Board of Trade accepting the Council's By-laws for the erection of overhead electric supply wires in their area. In the By-laws the height of the wires was set at a minimum of 30 feet. It seems that the tramway had erected supply wires at less than this height and they had asked the Council for a five-year period of grace before the wires had to be re-erected. The Council decided that one year would be appropriate.

The Sixth Annual General Meeting of the tramway Company was held in April 1904. The chairman, Mr W. L. Magden, said that the sale of power from the electrical generation side of the Company had improved greatly. Originally sales of electrical power in Kidderminster had been slower than hoped, but now they were better. The Company had made a thousand pounds more profit than the previous year, despite poorer weather affecting Bank Holiday business.

The tramway Company took a publicity initiative by printing a booklet describing the town of Stourport and its attractions. There were photographs of the town and a prominent part of the booklet detailed the tramway timetable, to enable visitors to plan their trip. The booklet was made available to intending passengers by application to the traffic manager. It also advertised joint tram and river steamer tickets (for a trip to the Holt Fleet Inn on the River Severn) that were available from the tram conductors.

In May 1904 the Councillors again turned their attention to the proposed Bewdley route. Councillor Mr Ray drew the attention of the Council to the fact that the time allowed for the building of the route to Bewdley was running out. It was his view that tramcars would be no more dangerous in the Bull Ring than the current horse and carriage traffic. Alderman Parry stated that the tramway Company had been asked to contribute £3,000 towards the widening of the Bull Ring and, while a letter had been received, the Committee had yet to discuss it. The Mayor suggested that the letter be read out. Some members thought, as that the letter had not been discussed in the Committee, it would be wrong to read it out at this point. Alderman Parry suggested that as so much had already been said it could be read out, but with no discussion. This was done and the response from the tramway Company was to decline to pay the sum requested. They stated that, as the road widening would be a benefit for the town, the Council should bear the cost, or allow the Company to run trams through the existing Bull Ring. The Council moved to the next business without any further discussion.

The 1905 May Day Bank Holiday was disappointing for the tramway. The Monday and Tuesday were busy with many visitors arriving at Kidderminster station and travelling on to Stourport by tramcar. However, the rain and cold wind on the Saturday depressed business, giving lower returns for the weekend, as a whole, compared to the previous year.

The view from Bull Ring to Vicar Street, showing the narrow section of road that the Council considered dangerous for a tramway service. Notice the 'ordinary' (penny-farthing) bicycles.

In June 1904 the Shuttle printed an editorial regarding the Bewdley tramway route, as the powers to build the line were to expire at the beginning of October. It said:

"It is now about four years since the tramway Company applied under the Light Railways Act for permission to lay down an electric tramway between Kidderminster and Bewdley. The Board of Trade sent down Commissioners to hold the public enquiry. The proposal met with very general support from the authorities of the two boroughs. There was, however, a very strong independent opposition, based chiefly on the difficulty that already attended the traffic through the Bull Ring. At two points the road is so narrow as to be, even under present conditions, a source of public danger. This danger it was said would be greatly increased if an electric tramcar service were added. The Commissioners, men fully qualified to consider the subject, after inspecting the locality, admitted the force of this objection. It was finally agreed among all the parties concerned, as the best way of meeting the difficulty that the Company should have leave to continue their present line from the terminus near Sir Rowland Hill's statue, Kidderminster, along Vicar Street, through the Bull Ring and on to Load Street, Bewdley, but that when made there should be no passenger traffic through the Bull Ring under existing conditions. The terminus of the Bewdley traffic was to be in Mill Street, near Mr Packwood's shop. In case, however, the Bull Ring should hereafter be widened, or even if actual experiment might show the possibility of so regulating the traffic that the tramcars could be run without becoming a peril and a source of danger, then the Council, with the sanction of the Board of Trade, might give consent under proper safeguards and guarantees. It was nearly twelve months after the inquiry that the Board of Trade issued the Order giving permission and imposing conditions for laying down the line, and the work was to be done within three years.

The Company, having obtained the Order and having accepted it with this precise and carefully prepared stipulation, from that day to the present, have not laid down a single yard of the line or shown any sign of carrying out what they undertook to do. When reminded of the obligation they incurred in accepting the Order of the Board of Trade, and that the sands are now running out, they do not attempt anything practical, but simply ask the Kidderminster Corporation to rescind the provision so carefully made by the Board of Trade, and which the acceptance by the Company was the very ground upon which the Order was granted. Nothing has changed all the conditions are the same. The Company has done nothing and attempted nothing. And now, ignoring all the considerations that influenced the Board of Trade, they coolly request the Corporation to forego the very cardinal condition upon the acceptance or rejection of which their application hinged in the estimation of the commissioners sent down by the Board, and as required by the Board itself.

The Corporation of Bewdley, representing the interests of the ancient borough, are naturally anxious that the work should be carried out before the time limited is reached. They appeal to the Corporation of Kidderminster to unite with them in facilitating the project. They have probably been told that the Kidderminster Corporation are throwing obstacles in the way, or are in some way responsible for the actions of the tramway Company. Nothing can be further from the truth. They are equally as willing as Bewdley Corporation to see the line made and communications facilitated between the sister boroughs. They have not thrown a single obstacle in the path since the Order was made. All they ask is that the Company do go on with the work they undertook, on the conditions laid down by the Board of Trade and to which the Company assented.

Views of the tramroad section of the tramway are rare. Here number 18 runs on the reserved track, on the left of the Stourport Road.

Tramcar number 24 at the Oxford Street terminus. Given the number of tramcars in the photograph (two double-deck cars and three single-deck) the occasion must be a chartered trip to Stourport. The photo has been used to publicise a local drapers (the advertisements have been superimposed on the photograph).

Suppose the Kidderminster Corporation were to do what the Company evidently wish to coerce them into doing – suppose they pass a resolution asking the Board of Trade to concur in rescinding the crucial condition on which the outside opposition was withdrawn and the permission to make the line was granted. What would the Board say? They would certainly refer to the original circumstances and conditions, and then ask "What has been done? What has changed?" and the answer would be "Nothing!" Except, perhaps, that the Company, for reasons of their own, no longer wish to go on with the work, and would like to throw the onus of their fiasco on others.

Let the Company push forward with the undertaking. The prohibition of passenger traffic through the Bull Ring can be withdrawn on only one of two conditions: (1) The widening of the Bull Ring or (2) a practical demonstration that the traffic is possible without danger to the public. The first condition is not to be had at present, for the Corporation cannot afford the expense and the Company declines to contribute to it. The second condition is only possible after the line has been made. If, when the line is laid, they can show by actual demonstration that the tramcars will be no danger to the Bull Ring traffic the consent of the Corporation will be granted at once. If the Company are really convinced that they will be able to give this proof, let them go on and finish the work. If they are not so convinced, they ought not to ask the Kidderminster Corporation to assist in removing a safeguard of the public."

THE BEWDLEY ARGUMENT CONTINUES

At the same time the Council debated the situation. In addition to the Bewdley route, which has been admirably summarised by the Shuttle, the Company was also criticised by the Council for laying an extra passing loop on Comberton Hill, by Kidderminster Station without bothering to get the agreement of the Council. There was already a passing loop at the top of Comberton Hill, by Farfield. It is thought that the new loop, beside the railway station, was built to take excursion traffic, allowing tramcars to wait in the loop for railway passengers while scheduled trams could pass on the journeys to and from the Somerleyton terminus. In regard to the Bewdley route the feeling was that the Company had the authority to build the line and operate it, with the proviso of not running a public service through the Bull Ring. They had made no effort to implement this authority and, while the Council would not make any obstacles, they could not use public money to subsidise the Company.

The Council formally discussed the issue at its meeting in July. To widen the road in the Bull Ring would require the complete demolition and rebuilding of the premises of Messrs Isaacs and Attwood. The Council had approached the tramway Company asking if they would contribute £3,000 towards the costs. The Company had said that they were unable to make any payment. In turn they suggested that the Council should retract their ban on any passenger carrying tramcars travelling through the Bull Ring. The Council could not recommend spending a large sum on widening the road, although they had no further comments regarding the running rights of the Company. Reaction among the Council members was very mixed. Some felt that the Company had no intention to build the line, while others pointed out that the current traffic, including steam trailers, motor cars and bicycles moving faster than the tramcars, did not cause problems. Indeed, one member suggested that tramcars would bring control onto the rest of the traffic. It was pointed out that the Company had known the conditions set by the Board of Trade when they agreed to them. They should keep their word. In the newspaper a couple of weeks later a letter appeared castigating the tramway Company for not adhering to the agreed conditions for the extension. "Pro Bono Publico" claimed that the Company considered the streets of Kidderminster to be theirs and they would soon insist that only tramcars could run on them! The author wanted the Council to oppose any application by the Company to extend the time limit for the construction.

The Bridge Street terminus in Stourport with number 10 having just arrived from Kidderminster. After the passengers have disembarked the tramcar will pull forward to the stub and be ready to make its return trip to Kidderminster.

A letter appeared in the Shuttle on 2nd July 1904 complaining about the tram rails in the town roads. The letter writer said that the rails were not level with the road surface, particularly in Oxford Street and Comberton Hill. This made them a danger to cyclists and other road users.

Also in July there was an accident. A tram was travelling along the Stourport Road late at night when the driver saw something bulky between the rails. He performed an emergency stop, but hit the object and when he got out of the tram he discovered that he had hit a man, Arthur Harris, aged 49. Harris was unconscious and badly injured. He was taken onto the tramcar and carried to Kidderminster where he was put on an ambulance and taken to the Infirmary. He was found to have serious injuries to his head and spine. He was operated on a few days later and was expected to recover from his injuries. However, this was not to be and he died a few days later. At the inquest a jury returned a verdict of accidental death. A little later in the month there was another road accident, however slightly less usual than others. At the end of July, a tramcar was travelling along Comberton Hill, near the Chester Road, when it encountered a herd of cattle and sheep being driven along the road. Although the tramcar was going slowly, three sheep were run over. Two died instantly and the third was so injured it had to be put down. The bodies of the dead sheep were so jammed under the car that it had to be jacked up in order to release them.

THE BEWDLEY EXTENSION BECOMES LESS LIKELY

The Bewdley extension was discussed by the Kidderminster Council at its August meeting. The Town Clerk informed the Council that a letter had been received from the tramway Company informing them that the Company was to request an extension of the time limit to build the line. The Councillors discussed the matter and felt that the Company would possibly build the tramway if things were favourable to them, or if not they would use the extension to prevent any other body from stepping in to build it. The Mayor said he was not in favour of stopping the Company, but felt that the Council should not object if the Company gave a binding agreement to lay the lines and have the tramway service running within the two-year extension. This proposal was accepted by the Council.

In October 1904, Isaac Smith was found guilty of being drunk and disorderly and of assaulting tramway Company staff. He had gone to Stourport and spent the day drinking whisky. Very much the worse for wear, he boarded the top deck of a tram bound for Kidderminster. He made a nuisance of himself and, as a tramway inspector was aboard the tram, the inspector approached him. After some abuse the man was asked to leave the tramcar. He refused and attacked the inspector. The conductor went to help and he was also attacked. The police were called and Mr Smith was arrested. The court fined him 30 shillings with the alternative of 20 days' hard labour, with no time to pay. His wife paid the fine and he was released.

Tram number 2 at the crossroads of Comberton Road and Chester Road, on its way to the Somerleyton terminus.

The Council received the decision of the Board of Trade regarding the application by the tramway Company for an extension of time to build the Bewdley line. Noting the concerns of the Council the Board of Trade allowed a six-month extension during which time the tramway Company was to reach an agreement with the Council. If they failed, then the powers would not be renewed.

A note was printed in the Shuttle from the tramway staff thanking the public for their generosity in contributing to their Christmas-box fund.

The year ended with a challenge to the tramways from the Great Western Railway Company. They announced a new rail motor car (steam railcar) service from Kidderminster to Bewdley (via Foley Park) and on to Stourport and Hartlebury. The Foley Park station was a newly built platform halt next to the bridge that the tramway ran over on the Stourport Road. This new service was unlikely to compete with the tramway, as the rail route to Stourport meant going to Bewdley first then reversing direction to take the branch line to Stourport. The time for the journey was 20 minutes and the cost was 4d. The tramway went directly between the two towns more quickly and cheaper.

In March the Council received a letter from the tramway Company expressing disappointment that the Council had not contacted them with proposals to enable tramcars to operate a service through the Bull Ring. They further said that without the opportunity to run the service through the Bull Ring they had no alternative but to abandon the project. This did not go down well with the Council, the members of which suggested that the Council write to the Company pointing out that the responsibility for the failure lay with the Company. To widen the Bull Ring would cost between £8,000 and £12,000 and the Company would not make any contribution to these costs and now wanted to make the Council the scapegoats. Finally, the Council decided to let the letter lie on the table (i.e. not take any further action).

The tramway Company held its Seventh Annual General Meeting in April 1905. Mr W. L. Magden chaired the meeting and he first mentioned the Bewdley line. He reminded the shareholders that the Company had an Order authorising the building of the tramway between Kidderminster and Bewdley, but under the conditions prevailing the Company could not carry passengers through the Bull Ring section of the line. This would have entailed passengers transferring cars with a walk between them. This was considered impractical and despite every effort it was not possible to persuade the Council to give permission to run the passenger service through that section. In the circumstances the Company would not be seeking an extension of the Board of Trade Order. In addition, the Great Western Railway had introduced a motor rail service between Kidderminster and Stourport, but the tramway traffic had not been affected by such competition (adding if competition it could be called!). At this time there were 43 staff employed by the tramway and electric power station.

The manufacturer's photograph of a GWR steam rail motor of the type that ran between Kidderminster, Bewdley and Stourport.

The GWR operated several local bus services in Worcestershire. This one started operating in 1905 linking Stourbridge, Hagley, Clent and Belbroughton. The GWR also had their eye on the Kidderminster to Bewdley route.

It seems that the tramway Company was unsure of the best way to run the service. Initially the two routes had been run as a single system, with trams going between Somerleyton and Stourport. This had been changed early on with the routes running separately Somerleyton to Kidderminster Centre; and Kidderminster Centre to Stourport. In 1906 the services reverted back to a single route.

The parcels service was another way of earning more revenue and advertisements were placed in local papers for the "Tramway Parcels Express". The main advantage being that the rates charged were lower than those of the railway or the Post Office parcel post. It also said that the tramway would collect parcels within a half mile of the tram route. Parcels could also be left with agents, three in Kidderminster and one in Stourport, as well as at the Company's principal offices at 10 Vicar Street. In April 1905 the tramway Company printed an up-dated booklet with description of the attractions at Stourport and a timetable of the tram service. This was issued free to customers on application.

For a while the Great Western Railway had been running a local bus service from Belbroughton to Stourbridge with great success. They announced in August that they would be extending the service to encompass a service to Bewdley, with four 1d stages in the route. They were planning to run ten journeys each way every day.

In September 1905 there was an incident in Stourport. A tramcar travelling to the river, carrying many competitors for an angling competition, came to a halt on the level crossing at Stourport station. The regulations governing tramways required that the live overhead wire should have guard wires set above and to each side, to protect the live wire from anything, such as tree branches, falling onto the wire and breaking it. On the level crossing one of these wires had itself broken and in falling had wrapped itself around the live wire, shorting out the current. Having lost power, the tramcar halted on the centre of the crossing, blocking the railway line and preventing the crossing gates from being closed. A train approached the crossing and had to be halted and both the tramway and the railways services were stopped for some time while repairs were made and the tramcar removed.

A week later Stourport celebrated a Land and Water Carnival to raise funds for the Kidderminster Infirmary and Children's Hospital. In the town, shops and houses were decorated for the occasion while many boats entered the spirit of the occasion with their own decorations. In a competition, prizes were awarded for the best decorations. Not to be left out the tramway Company encouraged staff to decorate tramcars for the event. One was reported as having over 200 coloured electric lamps. At the judging car number 19 was awarded first prize in the tramcar section and the team of staff responsible was given 10s 6d and cars numbers 24 and 9 were declared joint second and their teams won 5s each.

Decorated car number 5 with its proud crew. The notice on the front identifies the occasion as a Land and Water Carnival. Alas this car was not among the prize winners.

In November the Kidderminster and District Electric Lighting and Traction Company Limited were granted a Provisional Order extending the Kidderminster Electric Lighting Order 1891. The Order authorised the Company to lay cables in the streets and across railways to supply electricity to Stourport and the Rural District and, perhaps rather strangely, their own tramways. Clearly the initial electrical supply to Kidderminster town was a success and the Company wished to extend their business.

In December the tramway Company announced that following many requests from passengers they would be operating a Sunday timetable (a twenty-minute service) on Christmas Day. This was a departure from the more limited service on previous Christmases. A letter in the local paper, on behalf of the tramway employees, thanked the public for their generous donations to the staff Christmas Box where £15 was raised, of which £1 was donated to Kidderminster Infirmary.

In February a meeting of ratepayers was held in the Crown Hotel, Stourport, to discuss the introduction of an electrical supply to the town. Mr Offor represented the Kidderminster Electric Company and he was invited to present the advantages of electric light. Mr Offor referred to a letter from 170 ratepayers to the Council to petition them to agree to a supply of electricity to the town. The Company had sought a Provisional Order from the Board of Trade and now wished to extend their area of supply. It was natural that they would want to follow their tramway route to Stourport. There was debate over the time limit for the compulsory purchase of such an undertaking by the Council. Mr Offor said that the Government had changed the time limit from 21 years to 42 years to enable Company to recoup the investment it made in developing the supply. This was followed later by a letter to the newspaper complaining that the question of an electrical supply to Stourport was being placed in the hands of the General Purposes Committee, where several of the members had interests in the competitive gas Company, including the Managing Director. It was the view of the letter writer that the Committee would approach the issue with bias. He felt that the debate should go to the full Council rather than a Committee with its predominant gas influence. At the Stourport Council meeting in May it was reported that the Provisional Order had been received and it set out the same conditions for Stourport as were applied for Kidderminster. Additionally, the Company had agreed to contribute £20 towards the Council's costs of opposing the Order. The Council's agent highlighted the changes that had been granted to the Council, including the period before they were able to compulsorily purchase the enterprise after 21 years rather than the initially proposed 42 years. The subject came up again on 19th May when the Town Clerk reported that a letter had been received from the Board of Trade asking if the Council would agree to clause 7 (this allowed to the Company to supply electricity from the Kidderminster power station, meaning that power had to pass from the area of one Council to another). It was decided that this was a reasonable request and the Council agreed.

A Kidderminster resident complained in a letter to the paper of the outrageous behaviour of a passenger on the 5.40 p.m. workman's car to Stourport. The man was drunk and disorderly, yet he was allowed to travel on the tramcar. The author of the letter said that this was not the first occasion he had witnessed similar events. A few weeks previously, a drunken man had boarded a car at Oxford Street. The writer suggested that the tramway Company should throw such people off the cars.

In the summer of 1906 the newspaper reported a spate of road accidents involving cyclists. These included two where the tramway was involved. The first was in July when Cissy Buckley cycled into the side of a tramcar when she was riding down Comberton Hill. She was lucky not to be injured. A month later Walter Stanley was thrown from his cycle when his wheel caught in the groove of the tram rail. He dislocated his shoulder when he hit the road. Dr Miles was called and he treated the young man, although the paper does not say it, he must have put the shoulder back in place, as Mr Stanley was able to walk home. The groove in the tram rail was involved in a more serious accident in the same month. About 40 members of the Mothers' Meeting of Tibberton had been on a trip out to Habberley Valley. They were conveyed in two char-a-bancs. On the return journey the leading vehicle was travelling along New Road when one of its wheels got caught in the tram rail groove, breaking the spokes from the hub. The vehicle collapsed, throwing the passengers to the ground. The passengers were badly cut and suffered internal injuries. They were given first aid on the spot and two of the ladies were taken to the Infirmary. After being bandaged, the others were able to continue to the station to take a train back to Droitwich. Later in the month there was another accident, William Lewis, an elderly man, was knocked down by a tramcar on Comberton Hill. Being deaf he was unable to hear the tramcar approaching and had walked into its path. He was taken to the Infirmary for treatment and detained. Unfortunately, a few weeks later he died from his injuries. At the inquest it was said that Mr Lewis had stepped in front of the tramcar from behind a steam roller, giving the tram driver no chance to stop before colliding with him. The jury returned a verdict of accidental death and added that there was no blame to be attached to the tramcar driver.

At the September meeting of Stourport Council the clerk read out a letter from the Board of Trade informing them that the Electric Light Order had been passed and so the electric Company could introduce electricity to the town at any time.

A tramcar waits at the Bridge Street terminus, Stourport, while in the foreground is a fairground and a café for visitors, while in the background factory chimneys dominate the scene.

There was another road accident involving a tramcar in September when a cart being driven by Thomas Sparry was overtaken by a tramcar. The pony became alarmed and backed the cart into the path of the tram, colliding with it. Mr Sparry was thrown out onto the road, where it was found he had badly injured his head and broken a rib. He was treated by a doctor.

In December the Shuttle printed a resume of the progress of electricity in the town. They pointed out that it was paradoxical, but the increase in the use of electricity had led to an increase in the use of gas. They put this down to the changing expectations of the public. The brightness of the electric light had led to users of gas lighting to improve and increase their gas mantles. In addition, there had been an increase in the number of gas cooking stoves. The paper concluded that although the companies appeared to be competitors, they had contributed to each other's prosperity. It was also commented that the tramway service was excellent, however, the traffic had not been sufficient to pay a good return to the Company. 1906 had been the most successful year for the Company who will be extending their power plant during the coming year. The carpet industry in the town was also starting to realise the benefit they would get from using electric motors to power their machines.

Left and below: A shop in Stourport that acted as an agent for the tramway parcels express service. The notice says K.& S.E.T.Co (Kidderminster and Stourport Electric Tramway Company) Tramway Parcels Receiving Office. It is not known what was attracting the crowd.

CHAPTER 5

NO NEW ROUTE TO BEWDLEY

THE TRAMWAY HAS A STAGNANT PERIOD

1907 started with the usual letter of thanks from the tramway Company employees for the generosity of the public in donating over £13 to their Christmas Box Fund.

By the beginning of 1907 it was clear that the proposed route to Bewdley had been completely abandoned. It was evident that the tramway Company had anticipated that the Kidderminster Tramway would have been a far larger enterprise than had materialised. Apart from the initial tramcars purchased at the opening of the tramway, subsequent tramcars were transferred from the pool of used vehicles from the BET Black Country tramways. There had also been changes in the staffing that reflected the financial conditions of the two parts of the Company. On the tramway side the staffing was reduced by 8 to 23, while the electricity generation side the staffing was increased by 5 to 17. All conductors were trained to be able to drive the tramcars and on busy days they would drive while temporary workers would be employed as conductors.

The tramway had an initial surge with high numbers of passengers and profitable returns. After a couple of years, the carpet industry suffered a downturn and this was reflected in a reduction in the number of passengers. The tramway was reliant on the holiday trade coming from Birmingham and the Black Country to support its income. Bank Holidays were usually particularly busy times and if the weather was unfavourable the takings of the tramway were badly hit.

The Annual General Meeting of the Kidderminster and District Electric Lighting and Traction Company was held in April 1907. The savings on the wages bill had helped the Company to improve the dividend from the tramway to £4,080, while the electricity generating side saw an increase of one third in the number of lamps supplied with electricity. In addition, the carpet factories were starting to realise the benefits of using electric motors and more were buying their electricity from the Company. The numbers of passengers using the tramway had not shown an improvement and the Company was targeting excursion traffic to increase its business. The chairman was optimistic that the coming year would show further improvements.

On 7th May 1907 there was an accident that could have had far more serious consequences. A tramcar was travelling from Somerleyton Avenue to the town centre. As it descended Comberton Hill, the brakes failed and the tramcar ran away. Councillor Phipps was aboard and became alarmed and decided to leave the tram. In jumping off the platform he seriously injured his leg. The only other two passengers, Mr and Mrs Rollings, remained in the car and, though shaken by the experience, were not injured.

Mrs Elizabeth Allcock, proprietress of the Half Moon Inn, closed up at midnight on 24th May to travel home to Bewdley. She was in her dog-cart, driven by her ostler, as they left the Inn, the last tramcar of the day was driving past. The pony became frightened and dashed in front of the tramcar causing a collision and Mrs Allcock was thrown out of the cart. Luckily she landed on the front platform of the tram with only slight injuries. She had narrowly escaped from falling under the tram and being run over. The ostler hit his head on the road and lost consciousness. The pony was injured and both vehicles were damaged. There was another accident caused by a cyclist getting his wheel trapped in the tramrail groove. Thomas Stephens was riding down Comberton Hill and was thrown violently from his bike. He fell to the road and knocked himself unconscious. When he awoke he said he was not seriously hurt and he was taken home in a cab.

In July the Council had its annual excursion and the destination in 1907 was Tewkesbury. The trip for officials, heads of departments and assistants started at 7.30 a.m. by chartered tramcar for the run to Stourport. Here the party went by boat to Tewkesbury. They returned the same way and arrived back in Kidderminster at 10.45 p.m.

In the letters section of the newspaper T. C. de la Hey wrote to complain about the tramway. He said he had boarded a tramcar at Foley Park, bound for Kidderminster town. It ran on the single track section and should have passed the outgoing tram at the Worcester Road loop. However, an outbound car had gone through the loop and the two cars met on the single track. The outbound car then reversed back to the loop, but the driver failed to turn the trolley pole. As a result, the pole had de-wired and snagged with the wire, breaking it, causing it to fall onto the road and pavement. A conductor moved the live wire using a wooden pole, so that it lay in the gutter. The conductor asked a bystander to keep members of the public away from the wire. The two cars then moved off towards the tram depot. Nobody from the tramway Company was left to warn people of the danger, and the wire was still sparking on the ground. The writer asked why one tramcar missed stopping at the loop; why the trolley was not turned when the tram reversed; and why none of the four officers stayed with the broken wire to keep the public from touching it. He had written because he had been told of similar incidents that pointed to a too casual attitude of tramway staff.

In October the tramway Company announced that they were making improvements in service and fares to benefit local workers. There were a number of workers who were on short time who did not need to report for work until 8.00 a.m. or 9.00 a.m. and had to either travel on the early worker's cars and wait to start work, or walk to work or pay the full fare. The tramway Company responded by saying that it was introducing a weekly ticket for 1s 6d that would be valid for travel on any car running on any day of the week. This was not to affect the current workmen's tickets. The Company also introduced a fare of 2d single or 4d return for anyone (not just workmen) on any workmen's cars. In addition, the route from Kidderminster to Stourport would be reduced to two fare stages, the boundary being the Firs. They were also intending to introduce a faster service to and from Foley Park.

A rather odd announcement was made in the newspaper for 9th November 1907. It was said that the tramway was introducing a Tramway Parcels Express. This service was introduced and advertised in 1905 and so the 1907 announcement is confusing. However, there is one possible clue in the declaration. It states that arrangements were shortly to be made for the interchange of parcels with the other BET tramways in Birmingham, Dudley and Stourbridge. It may have been this expansion of the service that prompted the advertisement.

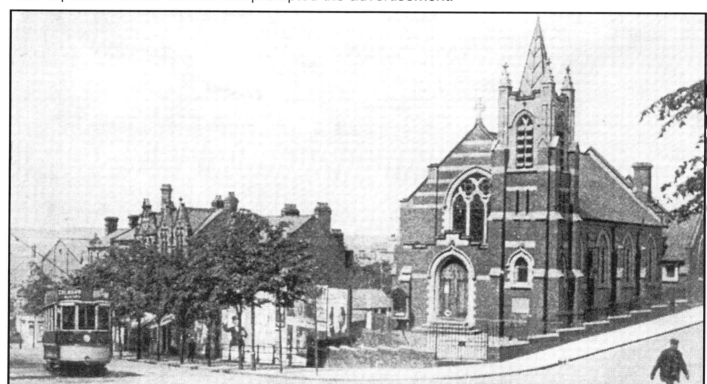

Tram number 2 climbs Comberton Hill (called Station Hill on the postcard). The imposing church on the corner of George Street was the Swedenborgian Church built in 1909 which was closed in 1960 and demolished in 1963. The site now houses a branch of Tesco Express.

Car number 19 pauses in Stourport High Street and the activity of the photographer has attracted a crowd, all keen to have their photograph taken.

In February 1908 the Board of Trade published their annual report on tramways in the United Kingdom. The Shuttle used it, and the corresponding report for 1878, to show the growth of street tramways in this country. The article compared the total route mileage from 269 in 1878 to the, then, current 2,394. Nationally the numbers of passengers had risen from 146 million to 2,455 million with net receipts increasing from £230,956 to £4,485,413, an increase of 20 times in 30 years. They then looked at the local Kidderminster system and found that for 1906 the gross receipts were £6,353 (made up £6,127 passenger fares; £84 mails and parcels; £142 animals, goods and others). A profit of £3,152 was declared with £2,560 going as dividends and £592 into reserves. The fleet was identified as having 13 electric cars. The Annual General Meeting of the Kidderminster and District Electric Light and Traction Company Limited took place in May. The chairman reported that the business on the tramway Company for 1907 had been the same as 1906, however, the electric generation side had a good year with a large and satisfactory increase in the use of power and light.

It appears that in May 1908 there was an issue between the Council and the Company regarding the overhead poles and wires on the Stourport Road, as it was reported that the tramway Company Manager had promised that the changes would be completed by the end of May, the Whitsun Bank Holiday.

On the evening of Wednesday 3rd June there was a massive electrical storm over the whole of the West Midlands. Torrential rain caused flash floods in a number of the roads of the town. As a tramcar approached Stourport it was struck by lightning; most of its electric bulbs were blown; and the controller was damaged. The conductor was filling in his way-bill when the bolt of lightening hit the car and the shock threw the way-bill out of his hand and it landed on the chest of a passenger. This upset the passenger so much he exited the tramcar and made the rest of his journey by foot. The storm also caused a problem at Foley Park where deep flooding stopped the tramcar service.

The Royal Bar-Lock School of Shorthand and Typewriting in Birmingham held their fourth annual excursion for over 100 pupils at the end of June. Travelling by train to Kidderminster station they boarded two specially hired tramcars that took them to Stourport. Here they boarded a boat for

Holt Fleet. After exploring the area and having a meal they returned the same way. A photograph shows the young ladies sitting on the tramcars at Comberton Hill, waiting for their journey to Stourport.

The weather for August Bank Holiday in 1908 was, for once, really fine with the Monday being one of the hottest days of the year. Visitor numbers were very high, with people visiting the area and staying for the whole week, not just the Monday holiday. There were many flower shows in the locality and all had record attendances.

Two trams wait on the loop on Comberton Hill for the ladies of the Royal Bar-Lock School of Shorthand and Typewriting, who were on their annual excursion.

One Saturday afternoon in October, there was an unusual incident that disrupted the tram service. Large tree trunks were being carried on timber wagons hauled by horses to the station for transport by train. The front part of one of the wagons broke away allowing the trunk to fall to the ground. Luckily the trunk (a huge elm) stayed attached to the rear part and did not roll away. However, at the top of Comberton Road, the street was completely blocked and trams were unable to reach the terminus and had to turn short, while other traffic was forced to edge around the damaged wagon. Although lifting gear was soon on the scene the recovery was complex with such a heavy load and it was not until late Sunday morning that the road was cleared.

November saw indications that the tramway was needing a more active maintenance regime. On the Stourport Road, near Oldington, the overhead wire became detached from its ear and hung down creating a danger that it may snag any passing tall vehicle. Urgent repairs were carried out. A few days later one of the traction posts in Foundry Street, Stourport, snapped due to rust and it had to be propped up until it could be replaced. Because of the danger of the pole falling, trams were not allowed to drive past. Passengers had to alight and walk to a car the other side of the pole to finish their journey. The damage was rectified and it is assumed that the tramway Company were prompted to undertake a survey of the condition of the overhead system.

A month later the swift actions of one of the drivers averted a potentially expensive accident. As the car was going along the Stourport Road the driver, Motorman Stone, saw a driverless horse and cart dashing along the road. Stopping his car Mr Stone leapt out and seized the runaway just in front of his tramcar, averting a likely collision.

The Kidderminster and Stourport Electric Tramway Co.

Tramway Parcels Express.

The fact of the frequent service of Cars on all Routes should appeal irresistibly to all business men, and shew at once the advantage in Despatch and Delivery of Packages sent by the T.P.E. Further, the Rates charged are much lower than the Rates charged by Rail or Parcels Post.

What this means in the course of a year to any Tradesman who sends a number of parcels is apparent. Say you despatch only 10 parcels per week or 520 per annum, and the average weight is 11-lbs.

The following will show the savings :

Cost of Despatch by Parcels Post :

	520 at 1s. each	...	£26 0 0
By Railway :	520 at 6d. each	...	£13 0 0
By T.P.E. :	520 at 3d. each	...	**£6 10 0**

The money in your pocket by handing the parcels to the T.P.E. in preference to Parcels Post is £19 10 0, and in preference to Rail £6 10 0. This is simply on 10 Parcels per week.

Again, the T.P.E. will collect your parcels. The Rates, including Collection and Delivery within half-a-mile from Tram Route, are :—

NOT EXCEEDING :	7	14	28	42	56lbs.
	2d.	3d.	4d.	5d.	6d.

There are Agencies at the following places and offices :

KIDDERMINSTER :
Mr. GRIFFITHS, Hairdresser, Station Hill.
Mr. J. BRAZIER, Confectioner, Oxford Street.
Mrs. Page, Newsagent, Foley Park.

STOURPORT
Messrs. HAYWOOD & SON, Printers and Stationers.

The Principal Offices are situate at 10, Vicar Street, Kidderminster

Any further information desired will be gladly supplied on application to the above. Telephone 108 Kidderminster

The advertisement promoting the tramway's parcels express service. The tramway offered the service for the delivery of local parcels and the advertisement illustrated the savings that could be made compared to the costs of using the Post Office or the railway.

In the usual tradition, the public contributed to a Christmas Box for the drivers and conductors of the tramway. Their thanks were passed to the community through the newspaper. The total collection amounted to £13 13s 2d.

The Board of Trade Report for the year 1908 for British tramways showed that the gross receipts for the Kidderminster tramway for the year ending 1907 were £6,373 (up a meagre £20 from the previous year). The profit for the year was £3,066 (down £86).

The Great Western Railway Company approached the Council to seek permission to raise the level of the Comberton Road bridge over its tracks. The Kidderminster Council had wanted to widen the bridge, but felt that the estimated cost of £300 was too much for them. So the Council saw this as an opportunity to ask the railway Company to pay for the road widening. It became clear that the railway would only pay for the bridge reconstruction if it was raised and the Council was not that concerned about the height of the bridge, but did want it made wider. This impacted the tramway Company because their tracks went over it. So the Council sought their opinion and clearly the wider road would assist their service without costing them anything. After seeking some safeguards regarding the widening of the bridge, the Council approved the request.

Mr A. Williams wrote to the newspaper suggesting that the problem caused by falling overhead tram wires could be minimised by placing protective nets under the wires. A couple of issues later a letter writer under the pseudonym "trolley" pointed out, rather sarcastically, that, being a genius, Mr Williams should design a trolley pole that would work with such a net. Mr Williams was not impressed and wrote to the paper saying that he had several practical methods of arranging a safety net that would not disturb the working of the existing trolley pole, however he did not elaborate upon them.

There was another accident resulting in a serious injury in April. Cyril Knott, a seven-year-old, had been standing behind a traction pole by Foley Park listening for a tramcar. When the tram arrived he ran into the road and unfortunately fell in front of it and its wheels ran over his leg. He was taken by the tram to the town terminus where a policeman took him by ambulance stretcher to the Infirmary. He was found to have a badly crushed leg which had to be amputated.

STOURPORT COUNCIL AND THE GREAT WESTERN RAILWAY

In July 1909, the Great Western Railway made another appearance in the story. People had been complaining to the Stourport Council that they often had to wait inordinate times at the level crossing while the gates were closed as trains went past. The Council approached the railway to ask if they would build a footbridge over the line to allow pedestrians to cross the railway lines safely when they were closed to road traffic. The response from the railway was that the delay to the public traffic was not more than at any level crossing. However, if the Council considered a footbridge was desirable the Company would have no objection to one being constructed, provided the cost were met out of public funds, to which they were a substantial contributor. This final sentence provoked laughter from the Council members. The station only gained a footbridge long after the tramway had closed.

In July there was a close call in Stourport. A tramcar had stopped by the Swan Hotel and a woman and her child alighted. The child crossed the road towards the Swan Hotel when a motorist whizzed along the Lickhill Road. The tram driver saw the danger and leapt out, seized the child and lifted him to safety, the motorist did not bother to stop.

As the winter approached, the Kidderminster Council contacted the Company to ask if they would erect a waiting shelter at the Oxford Street terminus as such a provision would be of great benefit to waiting passengers, particularly workmen travelling on the 5.30 a.m. tramcar. This request had originally been made the previous May. At the same meeting the Council were told that the Company had, in order to encourage more traffic, changed the fares to be more in harmony with what was termed a "Fair Fare system". But no details were given. These were printed in the 27th November 1909 issue of the Shuttle. Under the headline "Concession to Tramway Passengers" the paper gave details of the tramway "Fair Fare" scheme. The existing scheme was for the route to be divided into large stages with the minimum fare set at 1d. Travel within a stage attracted the stage fare. This rose immediately a passenger crossed into a second stage, paying for two stages. The tramway Company said that this meant that many passengers boarding or alighting by the stage limit would walk in order to reduce their ride to one stage. It was said that the new arrangement was to be introduced across the country and consisted of splitting the route into farthing stages, all of an equal length. The minimum fare would continue to be 1d, but travel beyond that would attract a farthing for each extra stage. To assist passengers, the traction poles at the edge of the stages would be painted white and black and have the stage number on it (the saying "beware of Greeks bearing gifts" comes to mind). The subject was raised in the January 1910 meeting of the Stourport Council where it was reported that the new "Fair Fare" scheme had been introduced and this had significantly raised the cost of travelling on the trams. One Councillor said that when the Council had originally agreed to the tramway Company laying its lines it was on the basis of an agreed set of charges and these had now been increased. The Mayor said that he believed that the tramway Company had authority to charge 1d per mile and the new charges were within that sum. A councillor said that if people boycotted the tramway he felt that the old fares would soon be reinstated. The Shuttle also reported that there had been many complaints from the travelling public over the new fare scheme. It said that the public were the losers at every stage, and that at some stages, it was said, the fares exceeded 1d per mile. They said that the tramway Company was claiming that there were advantages for the public, but the users had to pay more. The paper reported that many passengers had heeded the advice of the Stourport Council to boycott the trams until the old fares were brought back. It was noted that the workmen's fares had not been affected. The Chamber of Commerce wrote to the Council suggesting that they address the concerns regarding the "Fair Fare" system and the overcrowding of the 5.40 p.m. car from Kidderminster to Stourport. The Mayor said that he was sure that the fares had increased and recommended that the issue be put to the General Purposes Committee.

At the December meeting the Mayor was able to report to the Council that a meeting had been held with the tramway Company and they were agreeable to building a tramway shelter at the Oxford Street terminus, if land could be found.

CHAPTER 6

HOW NOT TO WIN FRIENDS AND INFLUENCE PEOPLE

LOSING FRIENDS

The Board of Trade published its Annual Report on British Tramways in January 1910. The Shuttle examined the returns for the local tramway. Comparing the year 1909 with 1908 the report showed that the number of passengers carried by the Kidderminster trams had been 725,209, a reduction of 68,008. The receipts were down £444 to £5,929. This was not the best of starts for the new decade.

No doubt the situation was not helped by the introduction on the 1st January of the "Fair Fare" scheme by the tramway, which to the travelling public just looked like a price hike and anything but fair. The immediate reaction to the proposals has been described in the previous chapter. Part of the route went through Kidderminster Foreign Parish and Councillors on the parish Council were getting many complaints from parishioners about the price rise. The matter was discussed at their March meeting. Whilst all the members of the Council were against the increases, the Chairman recommended that they do nothing for the moment as the issue was being raised with the tramway Company by the Kidderminster town Council and the Chamber of Commerce was also objecting to the scheme. If these two actions did not lead to redress, then the parish Council could take up the issue. A few days later the Stourport Urban District Council also met and discussed the fares policy. The chairman told the meeting that they had received a response from the Board of Trade, who considered that the tramway Company had the power to rearrange their fares without the Board's sanction. So the Chairman recommended that the Council write to the tramway Company to protest about the rise in fares. At the following meeting in April the Stourport Council reported that they had received a letter from the tramway Company stating that they "Could not revert to the old system of fares, as suggested by the Council." The general stance of the Company was that this was a modification to the fare scheme and not a price increase. The later returns to the Board of Trade demonstrated this was not exactly correct, as, although passenger numbers decreased after the new fare scheme, the receipts (and hence profits) rose. The passengers were justified in their gripe.

The weather during the Easter holidays in 1910 was delightful, encouraging a large number of visitors to the area. Many travelled by tram to Stourport from Kidderminster railway station and the pleasure boats on the River Severn were well patronised.

In April 1910 the Kidderminster Council contacted the Great Western Railway again regarding the Comberton Hill railway bridge, as it was no longer suitable for the increased amount of road traffic. The GWR agreed to reconstruct the whole of the bridge and increase its width to at least 42 feet, while carrying out their wish to raise the height.

King Edward VII died on 6th May 1910 and the country was in mourning. This placed a cloud over the Whitsun Holidays (on 16th of the month). When he ascended to the throne, King George V had indicated that people should continue to enjoy the Holiday. Though the atmosphere was subdued, the public still took the opportunity at the weekend to travel, with plenty using the tramway to visit Stourport.

In June, Alderman Brinton again raised the issue that was close to his heart, the building of a shelter for passengers waiting for a tramcar at the Oxford Street tram terminus. He suggested that the cost would not be great, while the benefit for travellers would be enormous, particularly as the winter was approaching. In September the General Purposes Committee reported that they had sent the tramway Company a plan of a proposed tram shelter to be erected on the footpath in Oxford Street adjoining the yard of the Green Man and Still Inn. The plan showed an open sided shelter on the pavement outside the yard. It was very narrow because the width of the pavement was very limited. It seems that there were second thoughts because a second plan was drawn showing an enclosed building set into the wall of the pub yard, with a seat around the walls. The plan shows it having a pitched roof, however, as built the shelter had a flat roof. It was 18 feet long, 10 feet wide and 8 feet high. The cost was to be £32 with a contribution of £25 from the tramway Company and the cleaning and lighting to be the responsibility of the Council. In October 1911, the newspaper was able to report that the shelter was under erection. At the beginning of November, the paper highlighted that many people were asking when the shelter would be opened, its completion was overdue and the weather had turned very cold and the shelter was needed immediately. In fact, the opening took place on 6th November 1911, without ceremony, and soon after the complaint about it being overdue. It was said to have ample proportions, two doors that were closed at night and it was lit by two electric lamps.

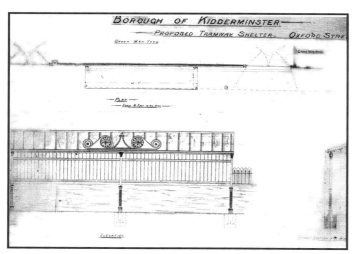

Above left: The first design for the tram shelter in Oxford Street.

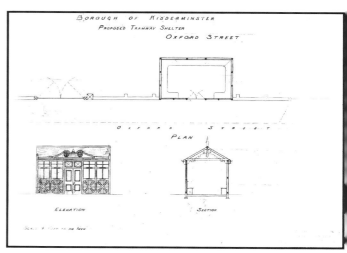

Above right: The Green Man and Still Hotel agreed to allow part of their yard to be used for the shelter and the new design was larger and offered more protection from the elements.

Above: This and that overleaf are the only photos found of the tramway shelter in the pub yard. This is an aerial view of the rear.

In July 1910 a party of visitors had hired four tramcars to take them from the railway station at Comberton Hill. The cars were parked on the loop waiting for their passengers when the combined pressure from the four trolley poles raised the live overhead wire to such an extent that it touched the bracket arm of the traction pole. To the excitement of the public there was considerable sparking. One of the drivers put on a pair of rubber gloves and rectified the problem. The report in the newspaper lacks detail and it is likely the driver went to the upper deck of an open tram and lowered its pole, thus easing the pressure on the overhead wire which would have dropped clear of the bracket arm.

The August Bank Holiday Monday saw a very large number of visitors. The railway station was extremely busy with nearly 9,000 passengers and had to operate until nearly midnight taking day trippers back home. The trams were also very busy taking several thousand visitors to Stourport. A second report about the trams indicates that many of the holiday makers were extending the Bank Holiday Monday as the paper reported that on the Wednesday one of the extra tramcars, put on because of the number of visitors, had collided with another tramcar at the top of High Street. Nobody was injured but one lady passenger was badly shaken and both tramcars damaged their fenders. August was the time in the year that many factories closed for their annual holiday and the area saw high numbers of visitors. The Shuttle was rather critical of one aspect of the tramway by telling the story of a visitor who was at the Stourport terminus at nine o'clock in

The Oxford Street terminus with a tramcar about to leave for Somerleyton. On the left of the tram-car the waiting shelter can just be seen outlined against the wall of the Green Man and Still Hotel.

the evening where a clock said that the next tramcar was due at a quarter to two. After waiting for half an hour without seeing a tramcar he asked a policeman why the trams were not running. The policeman told him there was a ten-minute service, but from the top of the High Street, half a mile up the road. The gentleman was one of many visitors who were misled. The paper rebuked the tramway Company for not placing a notice to show that the tram service was terminating short of the full route. They said it was fine for the local passengers, as they were aware of this vagary, but for the visitor from out of the area it was confusing, particularly if they had a tired family to manage and a train to catch.

The problem of delays caused by the Stourport station level crossing was raised again in September 1910. A hop pickers Special train had arrived at lunchtime, an hour late, and needed to be unloaded quickly to allow a scheduled passenger train to pass through. The Special train was too long for the platform and so one part was unloaded and the train drawn forward to unload the remainder. In doing so it was stopped over the level crossing, preventing traffic and pedestrians from getting across the track. Many workers were late getting back to their work and found the work gates locked (it was the practice for factories to lock their gates at the start time morning and afternoon, this lasted half an hour meaning that late workers lost half an hour's pay). On this occasion once the situation had been explained the factories allowed them in. However, the attitude of the railway Company was that the delay was unavoidable. The railway Company agreed that work was to be done at the station, but they intimated that it was just to widen (and not lengthen) the platform. The matter was raised at the November meeting of the Stourport Council. It was said that after the hop pickers episode the Council had received a letter from the local stationmaster saying that the hop pickers situation was exceptional and everything would be done to prevent a repetition of the situation. A Councillor reported to the Council that a few weeks previously a train had blocked the road and then on the Sunday the gates had been closed for 13 minutes. There had also been many complaints of the gates being closed for five or more minutes. A member suggested that the railway should build a bridge at their own cost. The Chairman reminded members of the reaction of the Council when the GWR surveyed the crossing to erect a bridge, when it was discussed one member caused the death of the scheme, reflecting the views of property owners in Newtown. There was discussion whether to take immediate action or wait a while. One member said that they should write to the Board of Trade to complain and that after three years on the Council he had never seen anything move too quickly yet. The Chairman reminded the Council that this situation had arisen because on the last occasion the Council was not unanimous, they need to show a united front. The issue was raised again at the December meeting of the Stourbridge Council when a report from the Special Committee was discussed. The report recommended that initially the Council should ask the GWR to lengthen the platforms and sidings, which would reduce the need for the trains to be stopped over the crossing. If no favourable response was forthcoming the Council could appeal to the Board of Trade. In fact, the railway put improvements in hand with plans to extend the length of the platforms by forty feet and the width of the up platform by seven feet. The work was scheduled to start after Christmas. However, at the January meeting of Stourbridge Council a letter from the Managing Director of the GWR was circulated. The Company stated that they had an official enquiry and the facts reported did not endorse the statements in the letter from the Council. The letter made no mention of any alterations to take place at the station. The Town Clerk said that he believed that the Company would be making the changes at an early date as it was reported that a high level railway official had told them that an order had been given for lengthening of the up platform. In February 1911 the newspaper was able to report that the platform at Stourport Station had been widened by six feet and lengthened by forty feet.

Just before Christmas 1910 a hole appeared in the road surface of Comberton Hill, beside the tramway line outside the Opera House. When it was examined it was found that the hole was considerably larger than first thought. The road was closed to all vehicles, including tramcars. The Council set about immediate repairs. It took three loads of material to fill the hole before it was safe enough for the road to be re-opened.

The Bridge Street terminus at Stourport.

Although the trams had been running in the area for twelve years some horses had not become used to them. In January Mr John Heath from Chaddesley Corbett was driving along Comberton Road when his horse became startled by a passing tramcar. The horse swerved to its left and the trap collided with a lamp post. The two passengers were thrown out and landed in the road. The harness of the trap was broken and the lamp post damaged, but no personal injuries were suffered.

LOSING INFLUENCE (AND PROFITS)

The 1911 Board of Trade returns for British tramways showed that the Kidderminster tramway continued in decline. The returns for 1909 and 1910 were:

	1909	1910
Gross Receipts	£5,929	£5,865
Working Expenditure	£3,397	£3,350
Passengers Carried	725,209	671,258

Advertisement for the joint tram and boat excursions to Holt Fleet and Worcester. This was a popular day trip for visitors.

Excursions to Holt Fleet & Worcester

THE KIDDERMINSTER AND STOURPORT ELECTRIC TRAMWAY Co.

ARE RUNNING

Combined Electric=Car and Steamboat Excursions

FROM

KIDDERMINSTER to HOLT FLEET, every Sunday and Wednesday, at 1s. Return.

KIDDERMINSTER to WORCESTER, on Wednesdays only, • at 1/6 Return.

Tickets can be obtained on any of the Company's Cars

The Saloon Steamers " Lady Honor " & " Beatrice "

Are Running in conjunction with these Excursions.

CARS leave KIDDERMINSTER (Oxford Street), 1.30, 1.45, 2.0, 2.15, 2.30 p.m.
BOATS leave STOURPORT for HOLT FLEET, at 2.30 and 3.0 p.m.
BOAT leaves STOURPORT for WORCESTER, at 2.30 p.m.
BOAT leaves WORCESTER at 6.0 p.m.
BOATS leave HOLT FLEET at 5.0 and 7.0 p.m.

The focus of the story now moves to the electricity generating side of the operation. The Board of Trade had written to the Stourport Council and the Kidderminster Rural Council informing them that the 1906 Order empowering the Kidderminster and District Electric Lighting Company to supply electric light in the two areas had not been implemented and the BoT were now considering revoking the Order. The Stourport Council were split in their view and referred the matter to the appropriate Committee. The Rural Council felt that another Company might be inclined to apply for an Order and they decided to reply that they had no observations to make on the matter. The Board of Trade wrote to the two Councils again in March to inform them that as no action had been made to supply electricity the Order was being dropped. The Stourport Council voted to write to the Board of Trade to say that they did not want the Order revoked.

The 1911 Easter holidays proved to be a record with increased numbers of people visiting the area, all enjoying the glorious weather. The newspaper claimed that one of the tramcars itself carried over 800 passengers to Stourport during the day. Many visitors stayed for the whole week. This was followed later in the year with a bumper Whitsun Holiday with hot and sunny weather that also broke records for the numbers of visitors.

On the 13th June an accident occurred on the tramway that could have had far more serious consequences. Two men were working on the overhead wire along Comberton Hill early one morning, using the tramway tower wagon. A tramcar with a working trailer was being driven down the hill by an Assistant Superintendent. Other workers were collecting disused wire and other materials and loading them onto the tram and trailer. Some Council men had recently watered the road and the rails were greasy. When the tram driver started the car down the hill he applied the brakes and skidded on the rails. Out of control the tram and trailer collided with the tower wagon and the two workers on it were thrown onto the road. One of the injured was able to be taken to his home, while the other was taken to the hospital and then was taken home. The report in the newspaper is infuriatingly vague and raises two questions. The first is the mention of a working trailer, which implies the tramway had a works trailer, however no other mention has been found, nor any photograph. Similarly, no photograph of the tower wagon has been found. However, it is likely that this was a horse drawn tower. The reference to disused wire, the use of the tram and trailer driven by an Assistant Superintendent and the time of day all suggests this was a scheduled replacement of the wire. Therefore, it is possible that the tower wagon and the tramway works trailer were borrowed from other BET tramway systems in the Black Country or Worcester. This could account why no photographs exist as they would only make rare appearances in Kidderminster.

The Coronation of King George V was held on 22nd June 1911. Stourport was, according to the report in the paper, lavishly decorated with flags and bunting. Crowds visited from the surrounding area and the tramway had to increase the service to a ten-minute frequency to meet the demand. Services of rejoicing were held at many local churches. There was a torchlight procession in the evening followed by a river carnival and fireworks display. Beacon fires were lit on surrounding hills while five fires lit up Hartlebury Common. Not mentioned in the paper, but appearing in a photograph, was a crossbench tramcar decorated for the occasion.

In July there was an unusual accident on the tramway. Janes Jones, a tramway engineer, was working on the overhead wire, the power of which had been switched off. So he was holding the wire without wearing rubber gloves. For reasons unknown, the power was switched on, badly burning Mr Jones. He was taken to the Infirmary and kept in for further treatment.

In the same month the electricity side of the Kidderminster and District Electric Lighting and Traction Company Limited approached the Stourport Council to ask if the Council were yet in a position to answer their letter sent in March requesting permission to supply electricity to the town using the overhead wire supply system. The Council discussed the matter and were concerned at the prospect of having many live overhead wires in the streets. During the discussion the Councillors realised that they had no technical knowledge of the implications of an electric overhead wire supply. So they decided to refer the matter to a Special Lighting Committee which needed to contact other towns that had such an electrical supply system to get their experiences. The report was put before the Council at the meeting in September, which found that there was no danger to the public from overhead wires. They had written to eighteen towns that were using the overhead wire supply system and had received thirteen replies. In some towns the wires had been used for twenty years or more. The consensus was that the wires were not dangerous to the public. There was only one report of any accident from a broken wire, and this was when a horse trod on a fallen wire. Many systems used a wire net under the wires to prevent any broken wire from falling to the ground. The Council decided that they would not object to the use of overhead wires and in October the Board of Trade deferred the question of revoking the Electric Lighting Order until the end of the year. In February 1912 the Board of Trade contacted the Council to inform them that they proposed to revoke the Electric Lighting Order so far as it related to Stourport, as they had received a letter from the Company stating that in their view it was commercially impractical to supply electric light to the town. The Board asked for the Council's observations. After some

A taste of what it was like in Stourport on a Bank Holiday when the crowds arrived to enjoy a day out. Horse drawn wagons (some looking like farm carts) load up with passengers for trips across the bridge and into the Worcestershire countryside.

critical comments on the actions of the tramway Company, the Council agreed to revoke the Electric Lighting Order and in March 1912 the newspaper was able to inform the public that the Board of Trade had revoked the Electric Lighting Order covering Stourport.

The tramway became the rescuer in the case of one road accident. On 12th August a motor car was driving along the Stourport Road away from Kidderminster. While going over the railway bridge the car swerved right to avoid an obstruction while braking hard. The rear wheels skidded and the car stopped sideways across the tram track with the front wheels over the edge of the embankment. One passenger in the car was seriously injured and the road was blocked. A tram-car arrived at the scene and using a stout chain was able to pull the car back onto the road and it was parked in a nearby field, though it was not until midnight that the road was cleared. The tramway was more directly involved in an accident the following month when a horse drawn spring trap was passing the Castle Motor premises in New Road, heading towards Kidderminster centre when it passed a tramcar going in the other direction. The horse shied and dragged the trap into the path of the tram. The two vehicles collided, damaging them both and causing the driver of the trap to be thrown to the ground. The driver was taken to a doctor but was able to go home later in the day.

At the end of February 1912 the coal miners in Britain held a national strike. The Manager of the Electric Lighting Company applied to the town's Magistrates to swear in the employees at the power station as special constables in order to protect the power plant as he feared the situation would be leading to tumult and riot and that ordinary constables would not be sufficient to protect the property of the Company. After listening to the arguments by the Manager, the Justices did not think that such an action was necessary at the time, however, the Manager could apply again on any day at any time if the situation changed.

The issue of the level crossing was again discussed at the April meeting of the Stourport Council. Councillor Bibb raised the matter saying that despite all the efforts of the Council the situation at the level crossing was no better. All members of the Council were in agreement and it was suggested that Mr Stanley Baldwin, who was a director of the GWR and who was born in Bewdley and lived in Stourport, should be approached as they were sure he would assist them. It was agreed that the Council should write to the GWR and to Mr Baldwin. In May the Council was able to report that it had received letters from both the GWR and Mr Baldwin. The railway Company would review the question of erecting a footbridge, while Mr Baldwin agreed that the subject should receive attention. In its 25th May edition the Shuttle publicised an example of the nuisance of the level crossing by saying that on the previous Thursday the level crossing had closed around 3.15p.m. and stayed shut for a considerable time, A queue formed of two motor cars, six conveyances, two cyclists, a nurse, a perambulator, various pedestrians and a tramcar. The gates did not open until the outgoing train had nearly reached Bewdley. The members asked if the GWR could explain why this was so. The Council had a reply in June when the GWR general Manager wrote to say that careful observations had been made at the Stourport level crossing and the result was that delays were of short duration and the Company did not see their way to incur the expense involved in the construction of either a bridge or a subway. Another letter had been received from the Board of Trade, responding to the letter sent by the Council. The Board of Trade requested details of the problems including the dangers created and the lengths of delay suffered by the vehicles and pedestrians. The Council decided that they should seek the information requested by the Board of Trade. The Council agreed that the clerk should write to the railway Company asking for the details.

Around the same time the Board of Trade wrote to the Council to inform them that the powers the tramway Company had to run the tramway were about to run out and the Board of Trade would be extending them by seven years. Later they wrote again to the Council to inform them that Colonel Yorke would be visiting the system to inspect it before a final decision was made on any extension. The initial letter was also sent to the Kidderminster Foreign Council who discussed the matter at their September meeting. The opportunity was taken to complain about the financial impact on passengers of the Fair Fares changes (Stourport Council had calculated that the new fares represented an increase of 25%). It was said that in the Black Country (another BET system) the tramways had been boycotted for a while in protest against the new fares system. The Council voted to write to the tramway Company complaining that the new fares system penalised residents of Foley Park and that the fare to the park should be reduced by a farthing to one penny (the councillors felt that the tramway Company had prepared the fares on a crafty basis). Stourport Council also complained about the state of the track and tramcars.

A quiet Comberton Hill showing the tram track but no tramcars. Most of the verdant trees have long gone and the scene today looks far less rural.

TIME TABLE.

During the Summer Season the Service will be run as under.

WEEK DAYS.

KIDDERMINSTER TO STOURPORT.

Cars leave Oxford Street, Kidderminster for Stourport at 4.55 a.m., 6.0, 7.0, 7.30, 8.15, 8.45, 9.15, 9.45, 10, and every 20 minutes until 12.0 ; then every 15 minutes until 11 p.m.

STOURPORT TO KIDDERMINSTER

Cars leave Stourport for Kidderminster at 5.25 a.m., 6.30, 7.30, 8.15, 8.45, 9.15, 9.50, and every 20 minutes until 12.15 ; then every 15 minutes until 11.30 p.m.

Oxford Street to Somerleyton at 7.55 a.m., 8.30 and every 15 minutes until 11 p.m.

Somerleyton to Oxford Street at 8.8 a.m., 8.38, and every 15 minutes until 11.10 p.m.

SUNDAYS.

KIDDERMINSTER TO STOURPORT.

Oxford Street at 9.20 and every 20 minutes until 1.0 p.m.; then every 15 minutes until 10.20 p.m.

STOURPORT TO KIDDERMINSTER.

At 9.50 and every 20 minutes until 1.30, then every 15 minutes until 10.50 p.m.

Additional Cars will be run as traffic requires.

An example of the summer time-table of the tramway for the time when the Stourport and Somerleyton routes were run separately with the latter not having a Sunday service.

The August Bank Holiday was a major disappointment for Stourport and the tramway. The weather was wet and depressing, indeed the river was so high that boating was considered unsafe. Conditions at the flower show were described as a quagmire. The newspaper christened the holiday as "The Black Holiday".

At its meeting in August, the Bewdley Chamber of Commerce resolved to write to the Great Western Railway to ask if they would run a motor omnibus service between Kidderminster and Bewdley. The Chamber said that there were between one and two hundred people who walked between the two towns each day as they had employment in Kidderminster. While the GWR ran a rail motor connection between the two stations, each station was located some distance from the centres of the respective towns. Motor omnibuses would be able to terminate in the centre of each town and the buses would also be able to pick up passengers from the settlements between the towns.

In September 1912 the Highways and Bridges Committee of the Stourport District Council recommended that, in view of the Board of Trade proposal to extend the running powers of the tramway by seven years, the district Council should cease the agreement that for £15 per annum the Council maintained the tramway track within their area.

Meanwhile in Kidderminster a new issue was being raised. A letter in the paper complained that on Sundays the tram due to leave Oxford Street at 12.00 a.m. was often late, having been held up waiting at the station for the 11.56 a.m. train which was frequently late. This caused inconvenience to church goers who were forced to walk in order not to be late for their service. In following issues of the newspaper there were two follow-up letters that somewhat confused the issue by criticising each other. There is no record of the tramway Company having taken any notice of the correspondence.

Colonel Yorke visited Stourport at the end of September to inspect the line prior to the final decision on the extension of the running powers. The Council had complained that the tramway Company did not run enough "Workmen's Cars" in the mornings (there were just two scheduled runs). The tramway Company explained to Colonel Yorke that if there was demand for more cars they would certainly provide them. However, on dry days many workmen cycled to work and it was only on wet days that the numbers increased. Colonel Yorke agreed that the Company could not run trams in case it rained. He also said that he could not make any comment on the fares that were charged. Councillor Evens, who was in the party accompanying Colonel Yorke, reported back to the Council that the Colonel did not think much of the complaints made by the Councils. It would seem that the tramway Company was not happy that they had gone directly to the Board of Trade. Mr Lycett, Tramway Manager, said that if the Council had any future complaints they should direct them to him and he would give them his fullest consideration.

THINGS START TO GET BETTER

The 1912 Annual Returns for Tramways gave the details for Kidderminster:

	1910	1911
Gross Receipts	£5,865	£6,418
Working Expenditure	£3,544	£3,449
Passengers Carried	671,258	705,769

This shows that the receipts increased a little, though the number of passengers was still below the 1908 figure. At the beginning of March 1913 the newspaper was able to announce that the tramway line between Kidderminster and Stourport was being renewed. Inclement weather meant that the trams often had to drive through pools of water.

June saw a welcome message for children and their parents, the tramway Company announced they would be introducing half price tickets for scholars using the tramcars. The month also saw a letter from Mr Stanley Baldwin saying that the GWR could not do anything about running motor buses between Kidderminster and Bewdley. In June the GWR had obtained authority from the County Council to close the level crossing in Stourport from midnight to 10.00 a.m. on Sunday morning 13th July in order to make improvements at the station that were hoped to solve the delays to road traffic.

Open cross-bench car number 9 was originally a trailer and then, in 1899, it was, with the other two trailers, converted to a motor tramcar.

Fred Tandy, a Councillor, wrote to the newspaper complaining that on a journey on a 'Workman's Special' he had been charged a 3½d fare, when other passengers on the tram had only been charged 2d. When he queried it he was told that these were the Chief Inspector's instructions. He then went on to say that the "Fair Fares" system had systematically squeezed the public. He gave as an example a passenger giving their destination as Stourport and being charged 3½d, when in fact had they said the Swan, Stourport, the fare would be 3d. He considered it legalised robbery. He was back in the paper at the end of August to say that the tramway Company had conceded his argument over the 'Workman's Specials' and that in future the fare would be a standard 2d. However, he went on to complain that while there was a 1¼d fare there were no 1¾d or 2¾d or 3¼d tickets and he claimed this was to enable the tramway Company to extract an extra ¼d from passengers. Interestingly he also mentioned that passengers could purchase weekly tickets, but only by personally visiting the tramway offices.

At the September 1913 meeting of the Kidderminster Council the Finance Committee reported that they had met with the tramway Company regarding starting a motor bus service between Kidderminster and Bewdley (the BET owned the Birmingham and Midland Motor Omnibus Company, better known as Midland Red buses). A provisional agreement was reached where there would be a bus service between the two towns; there would be two workmen's journeys both morning and evening; the price for workmen's tickets would be 1s 6d for a weekly ticket; if the workmen's buses ran at a loss the Council would subsidise it up to £200 per annum. The Council also agreed to give the tramway Company a monopoly on such a service. The news of this prompted two letters to the paper both objecting to the idea of the Council subsidising the tramway Company. The Company revised their offer and withdrew the clause regarding the subsidy of the workmen's buses. In view of this the Council agreed for them to go ahead. In October the paper reported that a London Company had also offered to run the bus service, on the same conditions as the tramway Company. Each was invited to give a demonstration of their buses with a run between the two towns. The newspaper reported that both demonstrations had been very satisfactory. After all the efforts by the Council and the tramway Company a 'Town's Meeting' was convened in October to discuss the bus service that had started without first having the prior approval of the town Council. Given the previously expressed wishes to have a bus service, the newspaper featured this as a Pickwickian situation. It seems that the Town's Meeting was called by the Council in reaction to the tramway Company having commenced the bus service without having approval from the Council or the police. The upshot was that the Council invited the

The New Opera House on Comberton Hill, opened in 1903

London Company (Allen's Motor Omnibus Company) to continue discussions. It was pointed out that by having two Companies involved a strong element of competition was introduced, leading to better terms for the Council.

There was a sudden change in the situation at the beginning of November when Allen's Company introduced a rival service to the tramway between Kidderminster and Stourport. To encourage patronage both the new bus service and the tramway reduced the fares, so the people could travel between the two towns for 1½d. Crowds took advantage of this and on Saturday and Sunday the transport was well used with folk travelling just for the fun of the ride. The Council met the following week and bowed to the situation. Licences were granted to William Percy Allen for six motor buses to ply for hire and to the Kidderminster and Stourport Tramways Company to allow two motor buses to ply for hire. The Council were aware that some buses had already been operating but had decided not to take any proceedings. They also recommended that the tramway Company be asked to forthwith carry out much needed repairs to the track. By the end of November, the price cutting war was telling on Allen's Motor Omnibus Company and they raised their fares to 2½d for journeys on either route, with three 1d stages on each. Before the month was out the Bewdley Council had received complaints from the residents about the erratic service of Allen's buses and asking that the tramway Company buses should also be licenced for the route. In response Allen's complained that their buses had been subject to sabotage. The Bewdley Council agreed to licence the tramway Company buses. The tramway Company had also applied to the Stourport Council for a licence to run buses. The Stourport Council considered that there was sufficient competition to Allen's from the tramway and decided not to grant a licence. At the end of November Allen's Motor Omnibus Company published their timetable and fare structure in the local paper. Finally, at the beginning of January the Kidderminster Council licenced the tramway Company to run seven of their red buses from Kidderminster to Bewdley, Cookley and Stourport, leaving from the Corn Exchange, the cab stand by the Co-operative Stores and Bridge Street respectively. The maximum fare for journeys to Bewdley or Stourport were set at 3d. and the routes would not have more than three stages set at 1d each. The Stourport Council had still refused to grant a licence for the tramway Company to run buses in Stourport (despite the fact that they were already doing so). As complex and involved the situation had become with unlicensed buses being run, it did mean that finally Bewdley had acquired a scheduled public transport service. But there was one more twist to this episode. At the end of January 1914 Allen's yellow buses were withdrawn leaving the tramway Company with a monopoly. By this time the tramway had purchased two buses and had a further eight on order. As a stop gap they hired eight buses in order to provide the service. Later in 1914 the buses were commandeered by the War Office. To keep the services running the Birmingham and Midland Motor Omnibus Company (Midland Red, also a BET subsidiary) stepped in to provide vehicles. The County Council entered the Stourport station debate when the GWR approached them for authority to extend the track around the goods yard. The County Council asked the Stourport Council for their views about this and the advisability of a footbridge. The Council debated the issue and were very concerned that they would end up having to pay for it. The final decision was to write to the County Council to press the importance of erecting a bridge.

Bridge Street, Stourport.

By the absence of a tramcar it is easy to speculate that this photograph of Bridge Street, looking down to the river and the bridge, was taken on a day when the trams terminated at the Swan Inn at the top of the High Street.

CHAPTER 7

WARTIME

WARS, NATIONAL AND LOCAL

In February 1914 Mr Charlton, the tramway Company Manager, left to take up the position of Manager at Sheerness and his position at Kidderminster was taken by Mr Wray, who had been Manager of the Tramways and Electric Light Works at Banbury. Mr C. S. B. Hilton resigned as Chairman of the tramway board and Mr J. A. Lycett was appointed in his place.

A major argument had occurred in September 1913 that escalated into a legal battle between Kidderminster and Stourport Electric Tramways Limited and Woodward Grosvenor and Company Limited. The case was heard in the High Court in London, on 30th March 1914. In August, Woodward Grosvenor, a carpet manufacturer, wished to lay a cable across Oxford Street to lay an electric wire to connect their factory that contained a generator, with premises they owned on the other side of the road. They contacted the Council to get agreement to lay the cable and were given permission. The tramway line to the station ran in the road. Woodward Grosvenor and Company commenced laying the cable on 2nd September, holes were dug either side of the tram track and a connecting tunnel was made to hold the cable. The cable was threaded through and the soil reinstated. The tramway Company learned of this on 16th September and they hired a gang of 41 men and transported them by tram to Oxford Street, where the tramcar stopped directly over the tunnel. The men alighted and interfered with the cable. The men were instructed to stay in the tram overnight. The next day the gang dug down and found the cable. The gang leader and another man started to cut through it. A policeman arrived and ordered the cutting to stop while he contacted Woodward Grosvenor and Company. A Manager from Woodward Grosvenor and Company arrived and tried to prevent the cable from being cut by jumping into the hole. The gang leader then instructed his men to start filling the hole, covering the Manager, who rapidly climbed out.

The issue ended up in the High Court. Before the judge the tramway Company claimed that the tunnel under the track had caused the track to subside over the next few days, dropping and twisting the rails. The track and foundations in that area had to be replaced and the Company was seeking compensation. However, an employee of the tramway admitted that this section of track had sunk prior to the tunnel being cut. It was the argument of Woodward Grosvenor that they had not damaged the tramway track. The Company had obtained the permission of the Vicar of Kidderminster as the road came under his Glebe and they had authority to break the road from the Council's General Purposes Committee. It was the contention of Woodward Grosvenor that the tramway Company was objecting to the laying of the cable because they wanted their partner Company, the electricity Company, to sell electricity to the carpet factory. Mr Lycett was the manager of both the tramway Company and the electricity Company and it was he who had instructed the men to cut the cable. Woodward Grosvenor knew that they would break the law if they interfered with the track, but by making a tunnel under the track, it would not be disturbed. Any sinking of the rails had occurred before the tunnel was dug. In reality the only purpose of the men hired by the tramway was to cut the cable. In addition, the 41 workmen hired by the tramway had fought with Woodward Grosvenor men in the excavations. This may have caused damage to the foundations of the track, but no evidence was given as to the state of the track prior to the fighting. Under the authority of the Court, Woodward Grosvenor were able to lay a second cable and the track above that cable had not been disturbed.

Prior to the laying the first cable, Woodward Grosvenor and Company had given notice to the tramway Company. Mr Lycett had contacted Mr Grosvenor (Manager of Woodward Grosvenor and Company) and to say that his electricity Company was seeking business and he wanted to supply the carpet factory with electricity. When he was refused he said that they were a big Company and they would see this through. The police told the tramway Company Manager to stop cutting the cable, but they waited until the police went away and instructed that the cutting should

Worcester Cross with the tramway running down into Oxford Street. Just past the London and Northern Railway Company building are the Woodward Grosvenor and Company premises which were the subject of the argument between that Company and the tramway Company over the laying of a connecting electric cable under the tram track.

continue and when the police returned the cable was cut three-quarters through.

In giving his decision the judge said that he found that the reason the tramway Company dug down to the cable was solely to cut it and intimidate Woodward Grosvenor and Company. When the police arrived, the tramway Company said that the police had no right to interfere, that was a monstrous attitude. The judge also found that the damage to the track and the concrete base had taken place well before the tunnel was dug. He found for Woodward Grosvenor and Company. They had claimed £28 in damages, but the action by the tramway Company was such that exemplary damages should be given and so he set the damages at £100 plus costs.

On 11th April 1914 there was a road accident that was reminiscent of silent films. A motor car was travelling beside Brinton Park when it encountered a tramcar. The driver thought there was sufficient room to overtake the tramcar. However, he discovered that there was not and the car ended jammed between the tram and the park railings. Luckily no one was injured but the vehicles and the railings were damaged.

The Bewdley Council reported that there had been many complaints from the public over the offensive smells emanating from the buses. The Council had asked the town clerk to draw the matter to the attention of the tramway Company and they now had a reply. The Manager had said that the smell had been created by a batch of faulty petrol. Members of the Council commented that the smell was as offensive now as it had been previously. It was also mentioned that there was hardship caused by the Company withdrawing school children tickets. It was decided that the Council could take action through the granting of licences on the price of the children's tickets but not about the smell.

The tramway Company advertised a new excursion in the area. They linked with two of the river steamboats to offer a joint outing to Holt Fleet. Intending trippers were told to purchase their combined ticket for 11d from the tram conductor. The tram would take them to the Severn River at the tram terminus on Bridge Street where the steamboats "Lady Honor" or "Beatrice" would take them down river to Holt Fleet. The boats left at 2.30 and 3p.m. on Wednesdays and 3p.m. on Sundays, returning from Holt Fleet at 5 and 7p.m.

The Easter Holiday in 1914 was a record for Stourport with heavily loaded trains, trams and horse brakes. The weekend went very well with only two visitors falling into the river!

At the end of May, the tramway Company published a new guide for the tramway. This covered not only Stourport and district, but it also extended as far as Bromsgrove, Redditch and the Teme Valley. The booklet was lavishly illustrated.

Life in Britain changed on 4th August 1914 with the commencement of the hostilities of World War 1. Most people expected that it would be over by Christmas, no one imagined that it would last until 11th November 1918. Initially there was not a great impact on the population, other than a recruitment campaign for the Army and Navy. Locally there was recruitment and training for the 7th (Reserve) Worcestershire Battalion, a home defense unit. The men were billeted in local private homes during their training. As the months passed the impact of the war became greater with the newspaper giving details of local soldiers injured or killed in action. Each week there were many such notices. Then prices of goods started to increase, particularly those relying on petrol and oil. Tramway and bus fares were raised. All these preoccupied people and there were less debates (or complaints) about the local public transport.

The 17th September 1914 saw a tragic occasion. Tram driver William Whaile, who had been a driver since the opening of the tramway, fell off his tramcar. The tram had left Stourport at 10.10 p.m. and as it left the passing loop at Oldington it jerked violently and the driver stumbled to the right. He tried to regain his balance by grabbing the vertical pole but was thrown off the tramcar. The conductor ran to the driver's platform and brought the car to a stop. He went back along the line and found Mr Whaile lying on the track. The conductor said that when the driver grabbed the pole he was swung in front of the dash panel and when he fell he was caught by the tram's lifeguard and dragged for some distance inflicting terrible injuries. When the conductor reached him he was dead. The conductor drove the car to the next passing loop and obtained assistance and informed the police. Later the track and tramcar were closely inspected and no defects were found. At the inquest, the verdict of the jury was accidental death through the man falling from the tramcar while it was in motion.

The generating plant in the depot power house. Demand for electricity from residential and industrial customers meant that additional generation power was needed, eventually resulting in the country's largest power station being built in Stourport.

Oxford Street with the Stouport route entering from the left along Bridge Street. A tramcar is just visible on the right, it is on the passing loop at the terminus.

Work on the widening the section of Comberton Hill by the railway station was completed at the end of October. With the new bridge erected by the GWR, the road had been significantly improved and the railway was able make changes to the station and goods sidings. There seemed to be a little problem with the road as in December the Council discovered that the tramway track was about six to nine inches too high. This led to traffic descending the hill keeping to the left of the track and when vehicles braked the wheels badly cut up the road surface. The tramway Company had written to the Council to say that to lower the track would cost £110 and this would have to be found by the Council. The Council debated the issue and decided that either the track could be lowered or the road and pavements raised. The problem was referred to the General Purposes Committee for a decision.

In November there was a direct impact on the public transport services when the whole of the bus fleet was commandeered by the Government for war duties. Midland Red supplied buses from their Birmingham fleet.

Two men appeared before the Borough court for using offensive language on a tramcar travelling from Stourport to Kidderminster on a Saturday night. Apparently it was common for drinking folk to travel to Stourport after the pubs in Kidderminster closed so that they could continue drinking. The mode of transport was naturally the tramway. However, imbibing first in Kidderminster then increasing the thirst by tram travel and topping up in Stourport tended to lead to excess. The tramway Company was not amused at having to take inebriated passengers on their return journeys, who caused annoyance to the other passengers by smoking and using offensive language. The court took a dim view of this type of behaviour and the two gentlemen were fined 5s plus costs.

Kidderminster Council had a contract with the tramway Company to repair the track within their area. This required the Council to undertake the maintenance of the track. The contract was coming to an end and the tramway Company had offered a three-year contract for £35 per annum. The General Purposes Committee recommended that the contract should not be accepted. However, the full Council accepted the offer.

The Board of Trade Annual Returns for Tramways was published at the beginning of 1915 and the details for Kidderminster were:

	1913
Gross Receipts	£6,369
Working Expenditure	£4,353
Passengers Carried	751,707

The figures were encouraging for the Company as they showed that the revenue was continuing to rise, as did the number of passengers carried.

Sometime in 1915 an extra double deck tramcar was purchased from the Birmingham and Midland Tramways Company. It had been built in 1904 by Brush, so was ten years old. Carrying its original number 15, it was purchased to help transport the increased numbers of workers who were occupied in the many factories converted to the production of munitions. There were also new factories built on the Stourport Road that attracted workers from both towns. Around the same time the four elements of the Kidderminster system; the Kidderminster and District Electric Lighting and Traction Company; the Kidderminster and Stourport Electric Tramway Company; the Kidderminster and District Electric Lighting Company; and the Worcestershire Motor Transport Company were incorporated into the Birmingham and Midland Joint Committee of Electricity, Tramways and Motor Omnibus Undertakings. Following on from previous practice the major repairs and overhaul of trams were undertaken by the tramway works at Tividale. A car needing work would have its body separated from its truck. The body would be loaded onto a low loader trailer and hauled by traction engine. If the truck also needed repair it was loaded onto another trailer and both trailers were hauled by traction engine to Tividale.

No doubt prompted by the winter weather in January 1915, the Kidderminster and the Stourport Councils' attention turned to their roads. In Kidderminster the condition of many roads, including Comberton Hill and Oxford Street was deplorable. It was said that the cost of keeping the roads well maintained was £400 per mile per annum. There appeared to be a particular problem on the tram routes. The tram track had granite setts, while the rest of the road was macadamised

Tramcar number 9 all decorated, though what the occasion was is not known, about to enter Lombard Street, Stourport, from Foundry Street.

(where the road surface was broken stones, not to be confused with tarmacadam where tar is used to bind the aggregate together). Under heavy and frequent use, the macadamised surface became cut up. In Stourport the concern was for Lombard Street, particularly as the tram track had been giving problems for some time. The tramway Company agreed to address the issue. In March the Stourport Council agreed to charge the tramway Company £10 to defray the costs of scavenging the tram track (keeping the road clean).

The Annual General Meeting for the tramway Company was held in May 1915. Mr Lycett told the meeting that the Company had sold the omnibus interests to the Worcestershire Motor Transport Company, an organisation of which the tramway Company held the majority shares. The services were hit by the wartime restrictions with the Sunday afternoon tram service being withdrawn on the Somerleyton route.

The 1915 Whitsun Holidays were the best for many years. The weather was sunny and dry with a glorious Spring. Due to war time restrictions there were no special excursion trains. Despite this, crowds came from Birmingham and the Black Country to enjoy the river and countryside at Stourport, many travelling from Kidderminster station to Stourport by tram. Some trams were reported as having 100 or more passengers. Returning from Stourport the queues for the trams stretched down most of the High Street. No doubt prompted by the crowds at the weekend, a Kidderminster resident wrote a letter of complaint to the newspaper. The evening journeys from Stourport were very crowded. He said that the crowds were disorderly with a large scrum of people and many being unable to get on the car. He suggested that a policeman should attend the stop and enforce a queue. As it was he and his wife were forced to walk up the track and catch a tramcar going to Stourport and then remain on it at the terminus so they could travel to Kidderminster.

In July the BET announced that they were about to link the power stations in Dudley, Kidderminster and Smethwick. At the same time the generating equipment was to be upgraded. When complete the three generating stations would be able to act as one unit.

In August the newspaper was able to say that the holiday period had been very successful despite some inclement weather. Large parties visited Stourport with many staying for several days. The tram service was well patronised with crowded trams going between the towns on a ten-minute service.

The Stourport Council again raised the issue of the level crossing. It was the view of the councillors that the promised improvements following the installation of new sidings had not appeared. Delays at the crossing caused by shunting trains were no shorter. On occasions they had experienced delays up to ten minutes and delays of three or four minutes were common. The delays had meant that some workers lost time and money on returning to work. There was talk of the GWR being sued by workers losing wages. Yet the railway Company would not build a footbridge over the line. The Council were also concerned by the withdrawal by the tramway Company of the workmen's weekly tickets. Now the workmen would have to buy daily return tickets. The Council considered this would create hardship for many workers. The police had contacted the Council to complain of the excessive waiting time by tramcars booked by special parties. On some occasions up to six trams would be parked in Bridge Street causing an obstruction. The police had suggested that the tramway Company obtain a depot where cars could park off the highway. This was considered an acceptable solution and the Council decided to write to the tramway Company with the suggestion. It was mentioned that the Council did not want to do anything that would discourage people from visiting the town. We can now look back and see that the tramway Company did not take up the idea of building a Stourport depot.

There was an incident on the Bewdley bus in March 1916 when Gerald Coles, a farmer, pulled the communication cord causing the bus to be stopped. When the conductor went to see why the cord had been pulled, Coles was abusive and used disgraceful language. The driver went to help and Coles assaulted both men. Coles was then ejected from the bus. Coles was charged with assault and appeared in court, where he said he was provoked by the conductor. However, he did apologise for his behaviour. He was fined £3 with 6s 6d costs.

WARTIME RESTRICTIONS BEGIN TO BE FELT

The World War had been going on for over two years and it was generally agreed over the country that the Whitsun holidays would not be celebrated in 1916. However, there were still large numbers of visitors to Stourport, though the length of stays was shorter and the activities were more muted than previous years. The annual fair in June was smaller than usual, the paper reporting that it was only a shadow of what it was in normal times. However, it was well supported and visitors, particularly the youngsters, had a good time.

The paper reported that, despite the wartime restrictions, a large party visited Stourport, arriving in six tramcars. As they travelled as a group there was difficulty at the passing loops. However, by inching forward it was possible for the trams to proceed on their journey. Indeed, in August the number of visitors was great, eliciting a comment from the keeper of a lodging house that, if this was the experience when holidays were barred, preserve us from the time when they are kept.

The August 1916 meeting of Bewdley Council debated the problems of the Sunday evening bus service. The number of people visiting the town at the weekends had increased significantly. They needed to return on Sunday evenings in order to catch trains from Kidderminster station to Birmingham. As the buses only ran hourly they were oversubscribed and people were left without a means of travelling. The peak time was between six and eight o'clock. It was suggested that the Council write to the tramway Company to ask if they would run two extra buses at that time. The response from the tramway Company was that there was a shortage of fuel, buses and of men to drive them. It was also suggested that the Council write to the GWR to request additional motor trains to assist the situation, but they had similar staffing and fuel issues. It seems that to keep order a policeman was sent to control the crowd. In the following year, in October 1917, a policeman was controlling the bus queue in Bewdley when Henry Gittens stepped out of his position in the queue and jumped on the bus as the first passenger. This created a rush and several ladies were crushed and a small boy injured. Gittens was arrested and appeared in court, where the policeman's evidence was corroborated by the bus conductress. The court took a dim view of Gittens behaviour and fined him 5s with costs.

High Street, Stourport with all the buildings decorated, though for what event is not known. Clearly everyone is wearing their best clothes.

The High Street, Stourport, on a busy day. Today the street is still a popular shopping centre with plenty of small shops catering for the needs of the Stourport folk.

Messrs. Burton, Delapole and Company, an ironworks in Old Hill, gave their employees a day out in Stourport in August. 200 arrived in the town by tramcars and they had lunch at the Crown Hotel before having a boat trip on the river. They returned back at 7.00 p.m. They just made the trip in time as the following month the use of petrol for excursions and pleasure trips was banned. In addition, street lighting had, on some streets, been reduced and on others it had completely ceased, so the streets were very dark at night. The lower parts of the unlit lamp posts were painted white to assist the road traffic. The reasons for the reduction was that there were Zeppelin raids over the whole country that bombed cities and towns.

The Stourport Council was still having difficulty getting anything done to improve the surface of Lombard Street. It reached an agreement with George Law, the contractor responsible for repairing the street track, where the Council would undertake the repairs in exchange for a payment by George Law of £28.

In November a passenger on a tramcar was seated with a large parcel next to him. The conductor asked him to move it, but he refused. The conductor then took the parcel and put it on the platform of the car, where he could pick it up when he completed his journey. This story made the local newspaper, which must have meant it was a very slow news week!

February of the New Year 1917 saw another increase in the bus fares, citing the cause as the increase in the price of petrol. There was an overall rise of 10%. Just two months later, in April, there was another rise, this time of a further 5%, again due to the shortage of petrol and, to compound the misery, services were reduced.

By now the number of road accidents involving tramcars had greatly reduced. However, some motor car drivers still seemed not to fully understand the implications of a stationary tramcar. Mrs Hardwick had boarded a tramcar in town and travelled up Comberton Hill to Lorne Street, where she alighted. A young man driving a motor car overtook the tramcar and knocked Mrs Hardwick over. She was taken to the infirmary with a broken skull.

The Whitsun Holiday in May 1917 was said to be the busiest yet. In Stourport boarding houses were absolutely full, with guests sleeping on rugs on the floor. Catering establishments were so full that private houses were serving meals. Every available boat was on the river, including privately owned boats that had been hired by desperate visitors. With so many inexperienced people in charge of boats it was remarkable that no serious incidents took place. The newspaper noted that among the visitors were well built young men, certainly not all munitions workers. It wondered how they escaped the net of national need.

In June the local paper adversely commented on the tram fares. They noted that the fares had been raised again. It had been 5d for a return journey, then the return tickets were withdrawn and the return fare became 6d. Now there was a 1d increase on that to 7d. It also commented that if a ½d fare were introduced to Kidderminster station considerable traffic would result.

The August Bank Holiday was another record breaking weekend with thousands of visitors descending on Stourport. Trams, trains and vehicles were packed with visitors. In the evening the queues for the trams went almost the whole length of the High Street and there was a similar length of queue at Kidderminster station to buy tickets. On busy days, particularly Bank Holidays, there would be chaotic scenes at the tram stops when hundreds of visitors wanted to return home. A correspondent to the paper cited the Bewdley solution of placing a policeman at the central bus stop to establish some order and suggested that there was a similar problem at the Kidderminster terminus. The disorderly crowd meant that the weak had no chance at all. A policeman would ensure that there was an orderly queue.

In September came the announcement that sugar was to be rationed. People had to fill in a form to apply for "sugar cards" giving them the authority to purchase sugar from January 1918. A few months later meat, butter, cheese and margarine were also rationed. This was on top of price controls that had already been imposed.

In the middle of October one of the tram drivers was very lucky. He was driving toward Kidderminster centre and was passing Foley Park, when the tramcar lurched and he was thrown out of the car. A passenger saw this happen and ran to the platform and halted the tramcar. The driver picked himself up, rather shaken, bruised and cut, but otherwise not badly hurt.

Another view of Empire Day in Stourport High Street.

Stourport Council once again had cause to complain again about the state of the tramway track in Foundry Street. The condition of the road surface was dangerous and although this had been raised with the tramway Company, no action had been forthcoming. The tramway now said that they had referred the matter to their contractor George Law. Meanwhile the Kidderminster Council were also complaining to the tramway Company. The Councillors had noticed that the staff of the Company were acting in a discourteous way. Frequently no notice was taken of requests to stop the car, leaving would-be passengers behind, sometimes passengers were refused entry even though the tram was only half full and cars would remain at the terminus and leave late, then run fast to catch up time. In addition, the Company refused to issue a timetable and became the only tramway Company allowed to run without a published timetable. It was agreed that the Company would be contacted in a vigorous manner.

To add to the constraints created by the war, the tramway Company announced that they would not be running any trams on Christmas Day. This was a common policy for all the BET run tramways in the Black Country. It was also announced that the BET would be seeking authority to build, beside the River Severn at Stourport, the largest electrical power station in England.

Some members of the Kidderminster Council were very concerned at the irregularities of the tramway service and it was generally agreed that the service was poor. It was mentioned that the Stourport Council were equally concerned. A proposal to write a letter of complaint to the tramway was deemed out of order by the Mayor. So Mr Tandy gave notice that he would move a resolution on the matter at the next meeting. It appears he had a change of heart, as no mention of the matter was made in February.

The crew proudly pose for a photograph with one of the first six tramcars to join the system.

THE WAR AND BAD WEATHER

There were several very heavy snowstorms in the middle of January 1918. Roads were blocked and the bus service halted. One bus to Bromsgrove took twelve hours to make the ten-mile journey. Schools were closed and the children had a fine time playing with sledges.

The condition of Comberton Hill was raised in the Council once again. It seemed to be a regular feature that the poor state of the descending side of the road was a cause of complaint. Heavily loaded vehicles had to use either a 'slipper' brake (a wedge placed under the wheels of the vehicle) or lock the wheels in place in order to safely descend the hill. This meant the wheels skidded down the road causing considerable damage to its surface. The Council Engineer was now having the top six inches of the road removed and replaced with new material in an attempt to rectify the situation.

In March 1918 there was an interruption to the service when part of the overhead line near the bridge by Foley Park became detached from its ear and it sagged down. The maintenance crew were able to make repairs, keeping the interruption to a minimum.

The tramway Company wrote to the Council in November to ask their comments on a revised set of By-laws for the tramway. The Town Clerk reported that he had read them and they seemed to meet the needs of the district. The Chairman commented that what was needed were some new tramcars as some of the present fleet did not seem safe to travel in.

Monday 11th November saw the end of the war. The armistice came into effect at 11 a.m. and the news soon reached Britain. In Kidderminster factories closed with workers thronging the centre of the town. Church bells and factory sirens were sounded. The Mayor addressed the crowds to formally announce that the hostilities had ceased and that services were being held in the churches to celebrate peace.

In the aftermath of war there were still price rises, particularly on motor fuel. The Omnibus Company gave notice that they were to increase the fares, again.

In December an irate letter appeared in the newspaper calling on the Council to take action against the tramway Company. The writer stated that the 5.30 a.m. and 6.30 a.m. trams had been cancelled and that the first tram to leave the station for the town centre was not until 9 a.m., far too late for business people.

Part of the reason for this anger is explained in a letter, sent in December to the Council, from Mr Bond, General Manager of the electricity Company. He assured the Council that everything was being done to improve the electric power and light in the borough. He apologised for the long stoppages on the tramway, explaining that by the end of the year the new plant would be in use. The members commented that the cuts in electrical supply had affected many factories, halting carpet machinery and causing much time to be lost. There was also adverse comment about the 5.30 a.m. and 6 a.m. trams on the Somerleyton route being withdrawn.

In time for Christmas, the Stourport Traders Association was able to announce that they had successfully gained concessions from the tramway Company regarding the penny stages in the town. The revisions were to be introduced very soon and would make travelling less expensive.

Over the wartime period the tramway generated a steady, if not exciting, source of revenue for the BET. The returns show the fairly steady increase in passenger numbers.

	1915	1916	1917	1918	1919
Gross Receipts	£6,166	£6,917	£7,332	£8,940	£10,333
Working Expenditure	£3,727	£4,259	£4,452	nk	£8,076
Passengers Carried	736,177	885,764	835,018	941,462	1,013,201

CHAPTER 8

PEACETIME

THE BEGINNING OF RECOVERY

While there were still many restrictions on the population, industry could cease munitions production and revert back to their original trades. The forces were being demobilised and soldiers and sailors were returning home to civilian life. The tramway was desperate for new tramcars as the original trams were now over 20 years old. However, the Kidderminster system was part of the Birmingham and Midland Tramways Joint Committee and no doubt the busier systems in the Black Country would feel they had a greater priority for new cars. So Kidderminster started getting second-hand cars to replace the very old cars. Two double-deck cars were purchased from the Birmingham District Company to replace double-deck car number 4 and single-deck car number 10, whose numbers they took. The Dudley Stourbridge system had a delivery of a batch of new Tividale type cars and also around 1918 sold double-deck car number 24 to Kidderminster (it retained its original number). The Kinver Light Railway sold Kidderminster single-deck car number 43, it was renumbered 3, the original number 3 being scrapped. Two double-deck cars from the Birmingham District Company were converted to single-deck and delivered to Kidderminster to replace numbers 1 and 2. Finally the tramway did acquire a new tramcar in 1921. Number 71, of the newly delivered Tividale type tramcars, became part of the fleet (it was renumbered 6 around 1923 when the original 6 was withdrawn).

Despite the previous apologies from the General Manager, Mr Bond, the complaints about the loss of electrical supply continued and the issue was raised again in April 1919. The Council had again contacted the electricity Company and had received a response from Mr Bond. He wrote that machinery was being moved from the Smethwick works so as to increase the local power supply. Members commented that a few days previously, the electricity cuts had forced 2,000 workers out onto the streets.

Mr George Wilson had an unfortunate incident with a tramcar. He was riding his motorcycle along New Road towards the town centre. As he neared Bridge Street he collided with a tramcar that was bound for Stourport. Mr Wilson was thrown from his machine, his head was badly injured and he lost consciousness. He was taken to the Anchor Hotel where he was seen by a doctor. He recovered from the accident, but his problems had not ended. He was prosecuted by the police for reckless driving. The court found him guilty and he was fined 20s with 10s 6d costs.

At its June 1919 meeting, the Council considered the proposal to enter into a contract with the tramway Company where the Council would maintain and repair the tram track for an annual sum. They also entered an agreement where the Council would employ a contractor to paint (with tar) the road surface around the tram tracks at the same time as the rest of the road was painted and the tramway Company would reimburse the Council for the element of work relating to the tram track.

The tramway Company was subject to some criticism when the Council received a number of letters from local workpeople complaining that it was charging excessive amounts for running special cars to Stourport and back. These were to carry private hire parties on a day trip out. The Company had quoted 1s 2d per person for the return journey. The clerk had written to the Company and the reply had just been that the Manager was away and they would write in detail on his return. When he returned, the Manager had visited the clerk and offered an explanation. The tramway Company had later written, agreeing to make some alterations to the pricing to make it more affordable.

After an inspection in June, the Board of Trade wrote to the tramway to say that "the need for repairs on a portion of track is beyond question". The tramway Company had taken action and George Law and Company had effected repairs that were then nearly completed.

In October the electricity Company applied to the Council to raise their prices because of the increases in the costs of fuel and labour. The proposal was to increase the charges from 5⅝d to 8d per unit. The Council were unhappy about the proposal and they voted to reject the request. Later the Company met with the Mayor and suggested a rise of 2d per unit. After discussion it was agreed that a rise of 1d could be applied immediately, then the position would be reviewed at a later date.

In November a gypsy cart was being driven up the High Street, Stourport, when a wheel got caught in the tram track. The rim and spokes were broken and parted company with the rest of the wheel. The cart gently sank to the ground without harming anyone or the horse.

In February 1920 the overcrowding of the early morning workmen's cars was raised again at the Council meeting. It was agreed that the Council would write to the tramway Company asking them to improve the transport accommodation for the working man. One member of the Council commented that the workmen's tramcars were so crowded they reminded him of the Black Hole of Calcutta. The Company replied in March saying that they would ensure that two of their largest tramcars would be used for the workmen's services. The Council hoped that this would make an improvement for the workmen. However, the Stourport Council was forced to raise the matter again in April because the difficulties continued.

Lombard Street in Stourport had been problematic for a long time. In February it excelled its inconvenience when, on cattle market day, it became blocked for a considerable time. A coal cart initially blocked the road when it was parked by the road side. Behind it was a huge bullock wagon followed by a van, a motor, and other vehicles, such that the tram service was unable to pass. No doubt passengers had to alight and walk for the remainder of their journeys.

April 1920 brought yet another increase in bus fares. The Mayor of Kidderminster did add that either the fares would be increased or the buses would be going on strike.

April also brought the Easter Holidays. There was a new attraction in Stourport, the opening of "Joyland". This enterprise seems to have been a mixture of a country park and a fairground. It was well advertised and visitors arrived by tram, train, bus, bicycle and all kinds of horse drawn carriages. The area was well fenced off, as visitors had to pay an entrance fee. Unfortunately, the

High Street, Stourport, well decorated, though it is not known what the occasion was.

Two crew stand in front of car number 2, one of the new Tividale design tramcars purchased from the Birmingham and Midland Tramways Joint Committee in the mid-1920s.

weather on previous days had not been kind and the path through the trees was a muddy quagmire. There were caves to explore, in one a fortune teller gave readings; there was also a coconut shy and a band playing for the entertainment of the visitors. On the Bank Holiday Monday there were over 9,000 paying visitors and a further 5,000 on the Tuesday. Despite the large numbers of visitors some of the side shows found that the takings were disappointing and they left the site. This was followed in June by the complete collapse of the venture with the whole thing being sold off by auction after a life of less than three months.

New generating machinery was installed in the Kidderminster power station (next door to the tram depot) in July 1920. The new items included three large boilers; a large alternator; and steam turbines. The capacity of the plant was raised from 1,750 h.p. to over 4,000 h.p. The cost of the new equipment and buildings exceeded £30,000. To meet the demand from the public, supply cables were to be laid to new areas in Kidderminster and (at last) to Stourport.

In 1920 the Government passed the "Tramways (Temporary Increases of Charges Act) 1920" that enabled tramways to increase their fares by application to the Ministry of Transport and if approved they could apply the fare increase without the need to go to Parliament for a full Act. What the Kidderminster Company sought was an increase of ordinary fares from 1d per mile to 1½d per mile and continue with the minimum fare of 2d and on the workmen's trams from ½d per mile to return tickets at 1d per mile and raise the minimum fare from 1d to 2d. An advertisement appeared in the local paper asking for representations to be sent to the Ministry of Transport. The Stourport Council decided to refer the issue to their General Purposes Committee to recommend if they should make an objection. A few weeks later the Kidderminster Council debated the issue and decided to contact Stourport Council with a view to sending a joint representation and had written to the Company with their objections. Later they discovered that the Company had implemented the fare increases without either informing them that the higher fares were being imposed or responding to their letter.

In September the tramway Company introduced an extension to their timetable. On Thursdays (market day in Kidderminster) the first trams were now to start from Stourport at 9.30 a.m. instead of the normal weekday start at 10.30 a.m. and run every 15 minutes. This would enable the folk from Stourport to travel to the market earlier in the morning.

The tramway entered the spirit of peace on earth and goodwill to all men when Mr George Cooper was prosecuted for using obscene language on a tramcar. The tramway Company presented the driver and conductor of the tramcar as witnesses. Mr Cooper did not appear, having sent his apologies. The Bench heard the evidence, noted that Mr Cooper had pleaded guilty. The Magistrates took a serious view of these events and recalled that Mr Cooper had appeared before them a few weeks earlier for similar behaviour. He was fined 40s with 10s 6d costs.

Agnes Wed was an unfortunate passenger on the tramway in January. As she alighted at the top of Comberton Hill her clothing caught on the tram and when it started she was dragged several yards along the road. The driver stopped the car and a policeman attended the scene. He found that she had some bruising but no other injuries and he took her to her home.

RECESSION AND STRIKES

1920/21 saw a steep recession in Britain. After the end of the war, production of munitions ceased and thoughts turned to restoring the infrastructure that had been neglected during hostilities. After a couple of years, the British economy had a sharp decline. It reflected a depression in America that effected production in this country. Production went down and workers were laid off. In the carpet industry there was a higher proportion of women employed than other trades, and they were usually the first to be laid-off. The local newspaper reported in January 1921 that unemployment in the area was still over 1,000. The local governments created a number of schemes to employ workers. Typically, these were relaying roads and building new houses. However, the Councils themselves were cash strapped and so initiatives were very limited. There was strike action in the building industry due to non-union labour being hired, which did not help the situation. There was also unrest in the mining industry where the pit owners were cutting the wages of the miners. Although the era is known as 'The Roaring Twenties' this applied to the upper and middle classes. Although employment did rise, many working families continued to eke an existence in poverty. The school leaving age was raised to 14.

Although many of the elderly tramcars in the fleet had been changed, the 'new' cars were almost as old as those they replaced. In March the Council had received so many complaints that the clerk was instructed to write to the Board of Trade in regard to the number of times the tramcars broke down and the irregularity of the service.

In March there was a serious tram crash. Two trams were due to pass on the loop near Oldington. The driver of the car going to Stourport misjudged his stopping and his car overran the loop. The tram bound for Kidderminster, driven by Reginald Rogers, was about to enter the loop and the two cars collided, one was described as a new car (probably number 71, a Tividale type tram). The fronts of both cars were smashed. Rogers was badly injured and was taken to the Infirmary where it was found necessary to amputate his left foot.

Looking down Bridge Street, Stourport, with a tramcar at the terminus.

Tividale design car number 10 (the fourth car to carry that number) in Stourport High Street.

The next month there was a report of another road accident, not directly affecting the trams, but giving an insight into the workings of the Company. Mr Richard Humphries, described as engineer for the Birmingham and Midland Tramways Joint Company (BMTJC), collided with a cyclist at the junction of Worcester Street and Marlborough Street. Mr Humphries was driving from Marlborough Street (now part of Prospect Hill) to Prospect Hill, while the cyclist, James Bowdler, had come down Comberton Hill. Mr Bowdler was slightly injured while his cycle was damaged. This is of interest to us as it suggests that BMTJC staff would often visit the Kidderminster Tramway to offer practical help and advice.

The Whitsun Bank Holiday in 1921 had a distinct air of gloom. The national coal strike had depleted stocks and the Government had applied restrictions. The Great Western Railway printed advertisements to say that the limited rail service would continue and no extra trains would be available for the Holiday weekend. The shortage of coal meant that the tramway Company had to announce that the Sunday service between Oxford Street and Somerleyton was to cease immediately. No doubt the Company were not too disappointed by this reduction of a service that yielded very little revenue.

By May the coal strike was having a serious effect on local industry. Many factories were on short time, while some had to close indefinitely, waiting for the strike to end. This meant that there was less money to spend in the shops and so they too were suffering. The restrictions on coal meant far fewer train journeys and therefore less visitors to the towns, particularly Stourport.

The strike had now lasted for 50 days and the lack of coal was having a serious impact over the country. The Government was doing its best to bring the parties together to start talking. However, the Mine Owners Association refused to meet with the Miners Union, being against the Union insistence for a national pool. The owners also said that they had no knowledge of any consultations with the Prime Minister.

The Whitsun Bank Holiday in May 1921 had brilliant weather. The very restricted train service meant that the number of visitors arriving by railway was down on previous years. However, that, and the fare increases that had occurred over the previous few years, encouraged folk to use their cars, motor bikes and cycles, as well as char-a-bancs and trams, to travel. While there were fewer visitors, there were more local folk staying close to home for their holiday, where previously they would have gone away to avoid the crowds. The procession and treats for the children still took place with around 1,800 youngsters taking part. Their procession was seen by cheering crowds. Overall the paper concluded that a good time was had by everyone.

The miner's strike ended at the end of May and this meant that there were many more visitors for the August Bank Holiday, though it was noted that most of them were day trippers. Around 4,500 went by train to Stourport on top of those that travelled by road.

The Council had received a number of complaints about the condition of the waiting room in Oxford Street. The oversight of the amenity was handed over to the Health Department. They arranged for it to be cleaned and thoroughly overhauled. The Council appealed to the public to keep it in good condition.

Around this time the price of coal was falling. The war having finished and strikes ended resulted in supplies becoming more normal and the high prices that endured during the shortage years were becoming lower as the mine owners took a more sensible approach. The tramway Company announced that they were reintroducing the return standard fare at a cost of 9d and 4½d for the workmen's returns. This was a welcome saving for the public. The local newspaper recorded that many people took the opportunity of saving 1d by buying the return ticket, but then by force of habit threw the ticket away, only to find they had to buy another ticket in order to get home!

Midland Red purchased some new buses and the local paper looked forward to seeing them on Kidderminster routes, as they were double-deck. The Midland Red operated over a wide area including the Black Country, Birmingham, Worcester, Kidderminster, Bewdley and Stourport. The Company had also published a handbook describing their services and descriptions of the towns that they served. It was on sale for four pence.

The serenity of a previous age is evident in this photograph of Comberton Hill, today the hill is full of parked vehicles and moving traffic. Alas most of the trees along the edge of the pavement went many years ago.

The Kidderminster tramway placed a notice in the paper announcing that as the temporary increase in fares was due to expire in February 1923 they were applying to the Ministry of Transport for authority to charge a standard fare not exceeding 1½d per mile with a minimum fare of 2d and the fares in the workmen's cars to be 1d per mile with a minimum of 2d for a return journey and 6d for the return journey between Kidderminster and Stourport. Representations could be sent to the Ministry of Transport within fourteen days. The Council debated this action and decided to write to the Company seeking assurances that they would not increase the current fares and would run workmen's cars until 8.30 a.m. The Stourport Council also discussed the application and decided to write to the Ministry of Transport to object to the application being granted. It seems that 1923 was going to be a disappointing year for the general public as, in addition to the rise in fares on the tramway, electricity was going to be more expensive with a rise in the cost per unit. The tramway Company was granted the temporary increase for twelve months.

THE BEGINNING OF THE END FOR THE TRAMWAY

The tramway Company wrote to the Kidderminster Council proposing major changes to the tramway:

Dear Sir,

(1) With further reference to your letter of 1st inst., and the interview which Mr Hilton and I had with you at your office yesterday, I trust we succeeded in conveying to you the impression that the Company is in no way wishful to be obstructive in the matter of your highway improvement on Comberton Hill. The directors, however, would prefer to abandon this entire route rather than incur any further expenditure on it. They are also anxious that, at the same time as we come to a friendly settlement in regard to Comberton Hill, we come to a settlement of certain matters of importance relating to the main line from Kidderminster to Stourport.

(2) The directors are doubtful of the utility of merely renewing the line as it stands today, and continuing the same standard of service as heretofore. What they have in mind is conversion of the line into something in the nature of a high speed electric railway, and to give a service between Kidderminster and Stourport considerably quicker and more frequent than the present service, and with a better fleet of cars. The past history of the undertaking has not proved encouraging but in the hope that the advent of the big electric Power Station at Stourport will result in an improvement in the traffic they are considering the doubling of the line from the Kidderminster boundary to the Stourport boundary, either whole or in part and/or the provision of electric signalling apparatus and other improvements.

(3) The undertaking however is purchasable on Tramway Act terms every seven years, and the next purchase date is next year (1924).

(4) We have recently had some pressure brought to bear upon us to "modernise" and lower the track above the Wrens Nest towards Stourport, inside the Kidderminster boundary.

(5) It would obviously be out of the question for us to put any considerable further amount of capital into this undertaking upon a tenure terminable every seven years, and without some certainty that we shall enjoy the sole occupancy of the strip of land that was purchased by the Company at its inception and upon which the line is laid. Any appreciable increases in speeds would not be granted to us by the Ministry of Transport if at any time the line was to become part of the general highway.

(6) The proposal, therefore, which I have to make is as follows:-

(a) The Company, with the approval of the Kidderminster Corporation to abandon the Comberton Hill route, the track of which shall be taken up by the Corporation, the setts and rails being handed over to the Company, and the Company contributing a lump sum in full discharge of all its liabilities in regard to the reinstatement of the road in the condition it was at the time when the line was constructed.

(b) The Company to throw (sic) certain portions of their track on the Kidderminster – Stourport route referred to above into the highway.

(c) The Company to be given a tenure of forty-two years from August 1924, and to be given the sole right of users of the strip of land by the side of the Kidderminster – Stourport route from the Great Western Railway bridge to the boundary of Stourport on which the tramway is now situated.

(7) I have also to add that in regard to the abandonment of the Comberton Hill route, the Company would, of course, remove the overhead equipment and make good.

(8) It would, of course, be necessary to secure the assent of the Worcestershire County Council and the Stourport U.D.C. to this proposition, but I feel sure that if the Kidderminster authority were prepared to support the scheme as here outlined, the other authorities would be prepared to fall into line.

(9) The whole arrangement could be embodied in an agreement between the parties concerned.

Yours etc
W.G.Bond
General Manager

The proposal was given to the Law and Parliamentary Committee for recommendations including that if the Company ceased using the Comberton Hill route, then they should pay the whole costs of the removal of the track and the reinstatement of the road and that the work should be carried out at times convenient to the Council. In regard to the statutory purchase of the tramway the Council would be willing to extend the minimum term to fourteen years. The Committee also recommended that an agreement should be entered for an alternative service on Comberton Road and improvement of the track in the Stourport Road. The Kidderminster Council asked that the tramway Company provide a bus service on the Comberton route, guaranteed for three years. The Company was only prepared to guarantee the service for one year, but if successful would continue beyond that. The Council was able to announce at the July meeting that agreement had been made with the tramway Company over the terms for the withdrawal of the Comberton route. The tramway Company had agreed to provide a replacement bus service for three years at a fare of 1d per mile. The service was to be at least the equivalent of the current tram service and there would continue to be no Sunday service.

Tramcar number 6 is about to climb Comberton Hill on its way to Somerleyton. The original Opera House was renamed as the New Opera House and then, as here, it was renamed the Royal Cinema De Luxe.

CHAPTER 9

A SHORT DIVERSION

ELECTRIC BARGES

The tramway depot was located on a patch of land that was defined by the River Stour and the Staffordshire and Worcestershire Canal. Access to the depot was across a bridge over the river while the canal was at the back of the depot building, which was how the coal was delivered. Beside the depot was the Electricity Generating Station. The tramway Company and the electricity generating Company were separate entities, but both were owned by the BET subsidiary the Kidderminster and District Electric Light and Traction Company (later it became part of the Birmingham and Midland Tramways Joint Committee along with the other BET Midland tramways).

The electric barge trial on the Staffordshire and Warwickshire Canal. The buildings behind the barge are the generating station attached to the tram depot. Photo Pathe.

In 1903 the BET incorporated the Shropshire and Worcestershire Electric Power Company to oversee the BET power stations within the two counties. By 1908 another adjoining County was added to make the Shropshire, Worcestershire and Staffordshire Electric Power Company. The Government gave backing to the Company to build in Stourport what was described as the largest electric power station in the country. Building started in 1923. At the same time the Company purchased an electric barge from the Gill Propeller Company of Kings Lynn.

The power Company had the idea that, as they were going to produce electricity, they could use it as the power source to drive electric barges along the Staffordshire and Worcestershire Canal to feed the new power station with coal. They decided to carry out demonstrations to trial the idea. As the electric power Company and the Kidderminster tramway were both subsidiaries of the BET, and as the canal ran along the backs of the depot and power house, this was a natural place for the trials.

In 1923 the electric power Company purchased a barge from the Gill Propeller Company of Kings Lynn. This Company was established to exploit the invention of Major James Herbert Gill. During the First World War he had developed a hydraulic propulsion system for special service trawlers. One application that was proposed by the Company was to power narrow boats on canals. The invention used an electric motor to power a shrouded propeller that generated a jet of water that powered the boat. The mechanism fitted in a wide tube that was part of the barge. This allowed

The barge passes under a bridge that still exists today. Under the arch the holes where the overhead wires were fitted are still visible. Photo Pathe.

the motor and propeller to be turned, rather like an outboard motor of today, but the Gill motor could be turned 360 degrees. Thus the motor could be used to steer the boat, eliminating the need for a rudder and if rotated 180 degrees it would act as a brake, slowing and stopping the craft. The boat could also be driven either forwards or backwards with equal efficiency.

At the demonstrations it was explained that this section of canal was particularly difficult, with many turns. However, it is more likely that it was the proximity of a friendly power station that settled the location, as the barge was powered through an overhead wire collection system. A double wire overhead was erected on a half mile long section, just like those used by trolleybuses (in those days called trackless trams). Rather than trolley poles, the barge was fitted with a wheeled, small trolley (called a troller) that ran along the tops of the wires. The 250 volt DC current was conducted to the boat by a loose cable. The electric motor and propeller drew water up from under the boat and then discharged it as a jet. An advantage of the system was that the whole motor and propeller unit could be easily removed and fitted to another boat in a few minutes. It was also claimed that this method eliminated any wash and the ensuing damage to the banks of the canal. The unit was able to cope with any rubbish in the water. Smaller items would pass through without impeding the unit. Larger material that obstructed the water inlet could be removed by turning the motor to the side where a cutter bar would clear the object away. Once the initial costs of erecting the overhead were met it was claimed that the running costs were one third that of using horses.

Demonstrations took place in August and September of 1923. The first was for Directors of the Shropshire, Worcestershire and Staffordshire Electric Company; the Staffordshire and Worcestershire Canal Company; and Councillors from the Kidderminster Council. In October there was a visit by the Executive Committee of the National Council for Inland Waterways. The visitors observed the demonstration and were then given an opportunity to travel in the barge. From photographs the barge appears to be a converted coal carrier, so the passengers had to stand for the journey. The barge starred in a Pathe Pictorial News film that was shown around the country. Indeed, it is possible to see this film today as it is on the internet under www.britishpathe.com (put in the search box 'electric barge').

The power station first generated power to the community on 2nd June 1927, when the tramway was in the throes of closing. The tramway service had been run down and by the time it finally closed in 1929 the only service was the early and late workmen's tramcars.

As far as the idea of transporting coal to Stourport by electric barge, despite the publicity, there is no record of any commercial use being made of this scheme.

Pausing between demonstrations , one of the crew is clearly on security duty, giving the camera man a suspicious look. The Company behind the trials "The Shropshire, Worcestershire and Staffordshire Electric Power Company" has its name prominently on the bows at one end (the barge could travel in either direction).

CHAPTER 10

BUSES TAKE OVER

THE COMBERTON ROUTE CLOSES

The tramway and bus employees had their usual annual outing and as in previous years it was to be spread over two days, to enable the transport services to continue to be run. The Fridays of 28 September and 5 October were chosen.

Mr George Law died in October and was buried on the 16th. He was a local building contractor and it was his Company that won the contract to build the tramway and then to maintain it. His experience on the tramway proved very useful as his Company won many similar tramway construction contracts around the country. They also built many large public works in the town and further afield.

The last tramcar ran on the Comberton tramway route on 31st December 1923. From 1st January 1924 the service was run by motor buses on a half hourly frequency. The change-over was a muted occasion without any ceremony. The trams quietly ceased running on the route and the buses took over. From the beginning of motor bus services in the town, the buses had used the spare space in the tramway depot to be stored and serviced.

In 1924 the temporary permission that allowed the tramway Company to charge higher fares, given by the Board of Trade, came to an end on 31st March. The tramway Company wrote to the Kidderminster and Stourport Councils to tell them that an application was being made to the Ministry of Transport to continue the higher fares. The Company assured the Councils that it was its intention to continue with the current fares and not to make any increases. In October, the tramway Company formally applied to the Ministry of Transport for a renewal of the temporary increase in charges as the current authority was to cease.

The tramway Company was still doing its best to get authority to build a passing loop on the track in Foundry Street, Stourport, but the Council were still opposed to such a loop, as the narrow nature of the road would make it dangerous. The Company had taken up the matter with the Ministry of Transport. They then asked the Council to ask if the Councillors would accept the decision of the Ministry of Transport as to the suitability of the loop. The Town Clerk had responded by writing to the Ministry of Transport pointing out that it was the view of the Council that the proposal was dangerous. A response was received in August in which the Ministry of Transport said they did not regard the proposed loop as dangerous and the stance of the Council was regretted. The Ministry of Transport hoped that the Council would reconsider their decision. It was decided to rescind the previous decision and to consider where a loop could be placed at their next meeting. The issue was debated again at the September meeting of the Council. The debate was mainly about procedural issues and it was finally decided that it would be raised again at the next Council meeting when it would be proposed that the tramway Company be allowed to build the loop. At the following meeting the proposal that the tramway Company be authorised to construct a passing loop in Foundry Street was debated. The reasons given for agreement to the loop included the views of the Ministry of Transport that the loop was not dangerous; the assurance from the tramway Company that it would only be used for two months of the year, during the summer; when it was used it would be for passing vehicles only, there would be no stop and no passenger would be allowed to alight or board the cars. The vote was equally split and it was on the casting vote of the Mayor that the motion was agreed.

James Perkins had a fortunate escape when cycling along Minster Road in May. The wheels of his cycle caught in the groove in the tram tracks and he was thrown onto a motor car. As a result, he sustained head injuries. The driver of the car, Mr Vale, took him to a local doctor who treated him. Mr Perkins was able to go home following the medical treatment.

The Swan Hotel at the top of the High Street, Stourport. The tramway would turn cars here rather than run to the Bridge terminus at the other end of the road.

W.T. CATTELL.   SWAN HOTEL.   STOURPORT.

In June 1924 there was severe flooding in and around Kidderminster and many properties and industries were affected. In Oldington the road was flooded and debris was washed over the tram tracks. It took several hours to remove the obstructions, during which time the tram service was disrupted.

Nationally the unemployment problem has been summarised as occurring in the early 1920s. However, in many industrial towns, such as Kidderminster, the downturn in the economy lasted through the whole of the 1920s. The local paper drew attention to this by printing the unemployment figures each week. For a number of years the Government gave grants to local authorities for job creation programmes for public works and Kidderminster had benefitted from this initiative.

There was a road accident in Stourport in August 1924. A lorry full of vegetables was driving up the High Street when it collided with a tramcar. The lorry was badly damaged and the windscreens of the tramcar were smashed. The flying broken glass injured two passengers who needed some medical attention. The road was covered in vegetables and produce making the street almost impassable. It was a while before the ensuing mess was cleared.

The Council was concerned about the tram terminus in Oxford Street. Since the Somerleyton route had closed there was no need for track to extend into it as the Stourport route cars were stopping in Bridge Street. What the Council wanted was for the terminus track in Oxford Street to be lifted and they suggested this to the tramway Company. The Company responded by saying that if they were allowed to extend the track in New Road a short distance to Marlborough Street (today the lower part of Prospect Hill) and there was an agreement that no competitive person or undertaking would be allowed to have passenger vehicles standing, picking up or setting down passengers in Oxford Street, they would agree to lifting the Oxford Street track, subject that the restrictions in Oxford Street were extended for ten years. The conditions were agreed and in October instructions were given to their engineers to carry out the changes. The result was a system with a single tram route that started in Bridge Street, Kidderminster and ended in Bridge Street, Stourport. It has not been possible to determine if the short extension along New Road was actually built.

In November 1924, the tramway Company re-laid the track in Lombard Street, with a passing loop, which meant that the road had to be closed to other vehicles. Luckily a new road had recently been opened that paralleled Lombard Street, called Vale Road. This allowed traffic to continue to flow. If the work had occurred before Vale Road was built, there would have been severe traffic problems.

There was an unusual accident in December when a tram was travelling along Minster Road in the morning in bad weather and dense fog. A traction engine with three trailers was travelling in the opposite direction and the vehicles collided. It is a testament to the strength of the tramcars that the traction engine was badly damaged, while the tramcar only suffered slightly. Indeed, it took two days to move the traction engine as repairs had to be carried out on the spot. Luckily one tramcar had been on the Stourport side of the accident. So a service was run from Kidderminster to the accident site and the single car ran a shuttle service from the site to Stourport High Street.

At the beginning of 1925, the Ministry of Transport sent the Stourport Council a copy of the revised Regulations and By-laws proposed for the Kidderminster tramway. The Council advised the Ministry that apart from one minor detail they were satisfied with the document.

The tramway Company ran tram and river trips during the summer, by arrangement with saloon steamers including "Beatrice", seen here just leaving its mooring station by the tram terminus at the bridge, Stourport.

October saw a repeat of the request to the Ministry of Transport to extend the temporary permission for applying the raised fares. In informing the Councils the tramway Company emphasised that there was no intention to raise fares, just to continue them at the current level.

The tramway Company now put forward proposals for a new stretch of track and a doubling of other parts of the system. Given the strictures of Lombard Street, the proposal was to lay a new section of single track with a passing loop along the new Vale Road. It would start from the existing tramway at the junction of Minster Road and Foundry Street, then run along Vale Road, with a passing loop just after the bridge over the canal. It would then turn right into Mitton Road, cross the canal again and join the existing tramway at the Swan Hotel. Here there was to be a triangular junction, that would enable the Vale Road/Lombard Streets to be used as a clockwise, one way turning circle. It was also proposed to double the track along the country section from close to the railway bridge on the Stourport Road to St John's Road. For this track doubling, the tramway Company would purchase a strip of land to widen the existing track bed, that they already owned. They applied to Parliament with a Bill to authorise the work.

The Shuttle interviewed Mr G. Chivers, the Resident Superintendent of the Kidderminster and Stourport Electric Tramways Company regarding the future of the Company. He talked of the doubling of the track along the country section. He said that all the rolling stock had been improved, in particular the old fashioned slatted seats had been replaced by spring seating (though this may have been stretching the truth somewhat as the open top cars were most unlikely to have had sprung seats, due to being exposed to the elements, while the new single deck cars had wooden seating, as seen in the preserved cars of this type at the Black Country Museum). All the passing loops had been fitted with automatic electric signals. He also mentioned new extensions of the tramway at both Kidderminster and Stourport. However, that in Stourport had been delayed due to that Council objecting to the extension. He emphasised that all these changes were proposed with the intention of improving the service for the public.

However, the national economy was not in a strong position. May 1926 saw the Trade Union Congress call a general strike in support of the miners, who had been locked out of pits. In addition, unemployment was high, and had been for many years. This had a severe knock-on effect for the tramway. Indeed, they declared a profit of just £19 for the year 1925 and this went very slightly higher in 1926 with £99 profit and back to £19 in 1927.

November 1926 saw yet another repeat of the request to the Ministry of Transport to extend the temporary permission for continuing the raised fares. Each time the extension had only been for one year. There were no objections from the Councils.

The Kidderminster Corporation expressed concern at the March 1927 meeting about the overcrowding that occurred on the one o'clock car from Kidderminster to Stourport, particularly on wet days and market Tuesdays and Thursdays. The members of the Corporation felt that the situation would be improved if the tramway Company would run a second car on those days. The clerk was instructed to write to the tramway Company on the matter. As if to relieve some of the dejection of the public during the 1920s, 1927 was a particularly nice Easter and the weather was exceptionally brilliant and in the country around Stourport the cherry and pear blossom was said to be a vision of beauty.

Stourport High Street is frequently busy with plenty of shoppers, however, the road is almost completely clear, something seldom seen today. Today the road continues to be a very busy shopping centre.

The dividend for 1926 was declared in June and was set at 22%, the same level as 1925. The majority shareholder was the holding Company, the Kidderminster and District Electric Lighting and Traction Company.

The closure of the Somerleyton tramway route was being felt by the people in the area, as a letter in the newspaper demonstrated. Using the pen name "Comberton" the writer complains that on market days there was no system of queueing enforced. Late comers rushed to the front of the queue, jostling and crushing young children and old people and the bus carried more people than it was licensed to do. The writer then commented that the Company undertook to supply an adequate service in place of the trams. He suggests that an extra bus be run on Thursdays and Saturdays.

At the Annual Dinner of the Commercial Vehicle Users' Association in April 1928 the Minister of Transport announced that all level crossings would be got rid of. He promised that any difficulties would be overcome by the Ministry of Transport joining with local authorities towards paying for tunnelling or bridging. This was reported in the local paper because of the long running issues at the Stourport level crossing. Clearly all those level crossings I have encountered while driving today must be figments of my imagination.

Albert James Law, age 50, was a most unfortunate man. He was walking beside the tramway at 10.10 p.m. on a Saturday in April, near to the sugar beet factory. A tram was driving towards Stourport and had stopped at the factory to allow a passenger to alight. After starting the car, the driver saw Mr Law ahead and he sounded his bell several times. Mr Law was close to the entrance to Glebe Farm, his home, and he stepped aside from the tramway. But as the tram got close he suddenly stepped onto the track and, although the driver applied an emergency stop, the tramcar hit Mr Law, who went under the front of the car. The lifeguard triggered the life tray, that dropped to scoop up Mr Law. The driver left the tram and walked around to the back. He saw Mr Law away from the tram track, but clearly very injured. He was unconscious and his head was badly cut. A passing motorist took the injured man to the Infirmary where he was found to have a broken leg. Whilst in the hospital he contracted bronchitis and died soon after. A verdict of accidental death was recorded.

THE END IS NIGH

The tramway Company wrote to the Ministry of Transport to ask for authority to close the tramway. The main reason given was that with bus competition the Company was finding it impossible to raise sufficient capital to carry out necessary reconstruction work as the Company did not have sufficient resources itself to carry out the work. The Company added that if the tramway was closed then the Birmingham and Midland Motor Omnibus Limited would operate an adequate service using their omnibuses, including the workmen's service. The Ministry of Transport wrote to the affected Councils asking for their response. The Stourport Council proposed a meeting of all the parties to discuss the proposal. In the meantime, the ordinary tram traffic on the Kidderminster and Stourport tramway ceased running on 1st December 1928, though the workmen's specials were to continue. The absence of trams prompted the Great Western Railway to apply for licences to run four buses from Kidderminster to Stourport and then to Bewdley and back to Kidderminster as a circular route. Clearly the other transport operators saw the end of the tramways as an opportunity.

Although the regular tram service ceased on 1st December 1928 the Kidderminster Corporation did not read the letter until their meeting on 12th December. The immediate feeling was that the tramway Company had been pre-emptive, something that irritated the Corporation members. In a very Corporation move it was agreed to put the matter to a Special Committee. It met in January and the first subject they decided on was that the tramway Company had no powers to pass over the rights to run a passenger service to the Midland Red. It was said that the tram services had been curtailed, not abandoned. The Council agreed that other bus companies should be allowed to run services, as the town would benefit from competition. One member did mention that as many as 104 journeys a day were being made along Blackwell Street and he expressed concern at the overcrowding this imposed on the roads of the town.

When the regular tram services were withdrawn, leaving only the morning and evening "workmen's cars", two of the 'Tividale' type tramcars were parked on the loop along the Minster Road to give room at the depot to house the replacement buses.

The prospect of the end of the trams led the newspaper to print a poem for the occasion (even though the end of the tramway had not been officially sanctioned):

Farewell, A long, a permanent farewell
   To you: you relic of a bygone traction.
No more we'll hear the clanging of your bell.
   Your lot is rest and rust and forced inaction
But there'll be ease in Foley Parker's joints-
The ease they missed when you bumped over points.

We'll miss you; you can bet your life on that;
   But then we've often missed you in the past.
Dashed to the terminus and gasped "My hat!
   I've missed it! And that bally tram's the last."
And other words and phrases without stint,
They'd "Parry-lise" our editor in print.

I loved those open top cars that had no doors,
   So trippers could observe the roadside charm
Of, say, the Sugar Beet! Or, in a pause,
   Inhale the fragrance of the sewage farm.
In many a garden cars will stand as sheds,
While even Tories ride with Midland "Reds."

Farewell (I'd better say it once again)
   Farewell, ye old faithful old electric steed!
You've got to go, for "current" can't retain
   Its place among our "current" transport need.
So history turns over one more page.
Yes, petrol is the "spirit" of the age.

However, this was slightly in advance as there was still a tram service being operated. The workmen's tramcars were still being run (as this was a requirement of the Act which gave the tramway the authority to operate). This was evident towards the end of January when a tramcar collided with a Corporation lorry at 7.30 a.m. The cause was a dense fog which prevented the tram driver from seeing the lorry that was parked across the track, unloading tarmacadam in the road. Thankfully no one was hurt in the accident.

No doubt those passengers that had been obliged to move from tram transport to omnibus were not at all amused by reading in the local newspaper in January that a Midland Red bus travelling from Stourbridge to Kinver skidded at Woolaston, hitting the verge and turning over. Around twelve passengers and crew were injured.

Meetings took place between the Councils and the County Surveyor. The latter wrote to the tramway Company detailing the conditions under which they would agree to the abandonment of the tramway. The Kidderminster and Stourport Councils were able to report at their respective meetings in March that they had received satisfactory responses from the tramway Company and so they would not oppose the closure of the system.

Ironically a report in the paper detailed a crash between the workmen's morning tramcar and a Midland Red bus on 20th March 1929. The tram was on its way to Kidderminster and it collided with the bus in the Stourport Road. Both vehicles were damaged but no one was badly injured. This must have been the last crash involving a Kidderminster tramcar as in the next issue of the paper it was reported that two tramcars had been parked on passing loops on the country section of the tramway along the Minster Road, by the Foley Park loop. The cars were Tividale type numbers 4 and 6 and they had been left in the open since Christmas to allow the BMMO Company to park extra buses in the tram depot.

The formal notification from the Ministry of Transport came in April, though effectively the tramway had been closed since 2nd April 1929, after the 5.30 p.m. service had arrived back at the depot. The end came without any recognition from the Company or the public. The first indication of the situation was when the Comberton route closed. Then the daily service to Stourport was taken over by a bus replacement service and finally buses took over the workmen's service. Apart from the humorous elegy in the Shuttle, the closing of the tramway went unrecognised. It did not take Stourport long to remove the tram rails from their streets. Within two months the newspaper reported that the lines had been removed from the High Street and Bridge Street.

The older tramcars in the fleet were scrapped in Kidderminster, but the more recently built Tividale cars were hauled back to the Black Country depot. They were probably offered for sale.

The new electric power station at Stourport, which, at the time it was opened in June 1927, was the largest in the country with a capacity of 250,000 kw.

However, given the recent closure of many BET systems in the Midlands it is likely that they remained unsold and were scrapped along with many other cars. The Kidderminster and Stourport Electric Tramway Company was liquidated a few months later, while the Kidderminster and District Electric Lighting and Traction Company changed its name in 1920 to the Kidderminster and District Electric Supply Company (itself purchased by the Shropshire, Worcestershire and Staffordshire Electric Power Company in 1938).

Thus ended one of the smaller tramways in Britain. At its start it was a pioneer system, the first to have tramcars with windscreens and the first overhead electric tramway system to be built from new (all the previous ones had been conversions of horse or steam tramways or used a different form of current collection). It had grand ambitions, but never had the capital to achieve them. In the end it faded gently out, apparently un-noticed by most people.

AFTERWORD

It is possible today to walk the whole of the tramway system and recognise most of it. Starting at the Somerleyton terminus the roads are virtually untouched apart from a few newer buildings. The first major change comes on Comberton Hill as there are now two railway stations. The platforms of the British Railway station are on the original site, while the former goods yard is now home of the terminus station of the Severn Valley heritage railway. At the bottom of Comberton Hill a large roundabout on the ring road occupies land that once was home for the Opera House. Beyond the roundabout is the Worcester Cross, presented to the town by John Brinton on 21st October 1876. At the town terminus the waiting room that was in the yard of the Green Man and Still on Oxford Street became a shop, with two others added either side. These shops and the hotel have long disappeared, demolished in the 1980s.

The Stourport route started in Oxford Street, and went into New Road, where there is now a mix of original and new buildings. The short road to the site of the depot is easily found, now called Tram Street (in the tramway days it had no name). The depot building and generating station have gone and an electricity sub-station has been built on the site. New Road leads to another roundabout on the ring road (actually only half a ring). Then the Stourport Road, past Brinton Park, is broadly unchanged. The road layout at the junction with Sutton Park Road has changed. The railway bridge survives, now over the Severn Valley Railway. In the tramway days it roughly marked the edge of the town, with countryside all the way to Stourport, with the tramway running as a tramroad on its own reserved track. Now the land between the two towns is almost completely built-up with just some farmland on the north side and the road has become a dual carriageway. In Stourport the railway station and level crossing closed in January 1970 and were demolished. The site is now residential housing. Foundry Street is now a cul-de-sac with only access for pedestrians from Minster Road. Apart from a few newer buildings Lombard Street, High Street and Bridge Street are very recognisable from photographs taken when the trams ran in the town.

Please note that in this book I have used the original street names (most of which continue with the same name). In particular I have used the official name for Comberton Hill, however, some may be more familiar with its local, unofficial, name of Station Hill.

A manufacturer's photograph of one of the first tramcars to run in Kidderminster. It has yet to be fitted with its trolley pole.

THE TRAMWAY FLEET

INTRODUCTION

This listing of the Kidderminster and Stourport tramcars relies heavily on the work carried out by Stan Webb in his researches into the "Black Country Tramways", supplemented by "The Tramways of the West Midlands" by W. H. Bett and J. C. Gillham revised by R. J. S. Wiseman. However, a postcard of another tramcar, number 19, that they had not recorded came to light in my researches and is discussed below. The initial nine tramcars were purchased specifically for the system. After that purchase, most of the additions came second-hand mainly from the other BET Black Country tram fleets. The Kidderminster system was not a high earning tramway for the BET and so was the poor relation when it came to new tramcars.

While minor maintenance and repairs were undertaken at the Kidderminster depot, any more complex work was undertaken in the large Black Country tramway depot and works at Tividale (between Dudley and Oldbury). As there was no direct track connection between the Kidderminster lines and the Black Country systems, tramcars moving between the systems would be hauled on a trailer, drawn by horses or a traction engine, to the nearest tram track, probably by the Stewponey Hotel at Stourton. The Tividale works would undertake major work, such as the rebuilding of car number 4 to a double-deck.

The history of the Kidderminster tramcar fleet is both complex and complicated and not helped by a lack of documentation, and existing records are often contradictory or shown as plain incorrect from photographic evidence. Only tramcars numbers 1 – 13 were new to the system (though even numbers 10 – 13 may have been second-hand). All subsequent cars were second-hand from other B.E.T. owned tramways in the Black Country.

Emile Garke was the managing director of both the Brush Electrical Engineering Company and the BET. So it was a natural move to purchase the tramcars for the opening of the Kidderminster Tramway from Brush, his other Company. Indeed, all the trams for BET tramways came from Brush, except in the early days (while the Brush factory was still expanding) when some tramcars were built by the Electrical Railway and Tramway Carriage Works Ltd., Preston.

This photograph was taken before the tramway opened to promote advertising. Boards were fitted to the roof to act as mobile bill boards..

THE FLEET

NUMBERS 1 – 6

The first six motor cars purchased for the tramway were Brush built single-deck cars that were delivered in 1898 ready for the opening of the line. These tramcars were an unusual design for a British tramway, being small four-wheel single-deck vehicles with totally-enclosed bodies. They were the first tramcars in Britain to operate with windscreens. They were fitted with Brill 21E type trucks and had the then newly introduced Brush type 800A four pole motors. Above the windscreens a headlamp was fitted each end, these were so small as to be virtually useless. Later in life the headlights were replaced with larger, more useful ones, fitted to the dashes, while the original headlights were removed. The cars arrived fitted with couplings in order to haul the open-sided trailers. The reason for the unusual design of these cars and the three trailers was that they had originally been ordered from Brush for use in Cairo and the contract had, for some reason, been cancelled and they were diverted to the far less clement weather of North Worcestershire.

A poor photograph, but the only one found that shows the original car number 4 (on the right) in its rebuilt, double-deck form. This is the passing loop at the junction of Stourport Road with Sutton Park Road.

The dimensions of the motor cars were: body length 16ft 10ins (27ft 6ins over the couplings); width 6ft 4ins; overall height 10ft 5ins; and a wheelbase of 6ft 6ins with a wheel diameter of 30ins. There was seating for 24 passengers. A small revolving destination board was fitted over the central window of the windscreen and advertising boards fitted either side of the roof.

Around 1903 car number 4 was rebuilt as an open-top double-deck car with reversed stairs. Number 4, and numbers 1, 2, 3 and 6 were scrapped around 1919 and the numbers allocated to second-hand cars from the Dudley and Stourbridge system, except number 6 that was replaced by one of the new Tividale design cars.

NUMBERS 7 – 9

The next three cars to be delivered for the opening were three open-sided crossbench trailers. Having similar trucks and roofs to the motor cars, the trailers could seat 40. However, they were ill fitted for the Kidderminster climate. The basic dimensions matched those of the power cars. It soon became obvious to the management that the line was not suitable for trailer cars and it could work more effectively if the three cars were converted to motor cars. The conversion took place around September 1899 and the cars operated as independent motor cars. The seating capacity was reduced to 36 (presumably because no passengers were allowed on the platform seats at the driving end, though photographs do show passengers sitting on the driver's plat-form). It is believed that in the early 1920s the cars were modified to give the passengers a little more protection in inclement weather. The west side of the cars (the hedge side on the reserved track) were closed in by panelling the opening to waist height with windows above. Access to the cars would then have only been from the other side.

Delivered as a trailer car, number 8 was converted to a motor car in 1899. The tram has two conductors, no doubt it is a Bank Holiday with large crowds travelling on the tramway. The conductor by the driver appears to be a permanent employ-ee (he has a Compa-ny cap and jacket) while the other is more likely a tempo-rary employee.

NUMBERS 10 - 13

At the same time as the original crossbench trailers were being converted to motor cars, four more open-sided crossbench trailers were purchased. Only one photograph of any of these cars has been found. They were smaller than the original trailer cars, two had seating for 24 passengers while the other two had seating for 16 passengers. In 1902 the cars no longer appeared on the fleet list of the tramway. It is intriguing to speculate on their origins and what the reasons were for both the addition to the fleet and why they lasted such a short time. Given the smaller size of the cars it is possible that they were actually built as horse tramcars. Also the number of electrical conversions taking place around the country leads to speculation that some BET tramways had surplus horse tramcars for disposal. At the time second-hand horse tramcars would have been at their cheapest. Once the original trailers were motorised they would become more versatile and the new trailers were possibly obtained for use at weekends, market days and Bank Holidays, when large numbers of passengers travelled to and from Stourport. It seems that, with the complexities of motor tramcars running around trailers at Somerleyton, Oxford Street and Bridge Street, the Company decided to cease using trailers and replace them with double-deck motor cars 10($_2$), 19 and 25 (see below) which would allow a more flexible use.

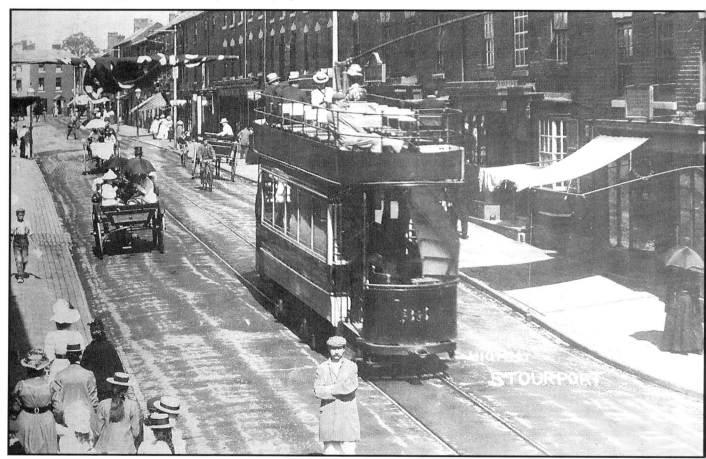

Tramcar number 25 is driven up Stourport High Street, on its way to Kidderminster. This was originally a single-deck car used on the Dudley and Stourbridge system.

NUMBERS 10($_2$), 19 AND 25

In 1900 the BET had ordered a large number of cars from the Electric Railway and Tramway Carriage Works in Preston. They were partially distributed around various BET subsidiary tramways, while some were held in store. In 1901 the Kidderminster management were looking for some extra tramcars and purchased three, two from the Dudley and Stourbridge Tramway (numbers 19 and 25 in the D&S fleet) and one (that was given the number 10, the original 10 having being scrapped) from the reserve stock from the BET. They were originally built as enclosed single-deck cars with five window saloons and four-wheel 'Lord Baltimore' American trucks. For use on the Kidderminster line the cars were rebuilt as open-top, double-deck trams with reversed stairs and a centrally located trolley standard, prior to delivery to the Kidderminster system.

They were fitted with couplings for trailer operation, though within a few months the system had disposed of their remaining trailer cars. The size of the cars was 18ft 2ins over saloon, 27ft 2ins over fenders and 28ft 8ins over couplers. The wheelbase was 6ft 6ins with a wheel diameter of 30ins and the overall width 6ft 2ins.

Number 10($_2$) was acquired in 1901 from the reserve stock held by the BET.

NUMBER 24

Later in 1901 car number 24 joined the fleet. This was another of the batch purchased in 1900 from the Electric Railway and Tramway Carriage Works. It too was rebuilt as an open-top double-deck car before delivery to Kidderminster. However, the design was somewhat different from the previous rebuilds. It had short canopies, direct stairs, 'Lord Baltimore' trucks and a side mounted trolley standard. Like the previous purchases from the Dudley and Stourbridge line it retained its original number of 24. It is believed that the direct stairs on the car were a pair from one of the three double deck bogie cars purchased for the Kinver Light Railway. The Board of Trade Inspector refused permission for any double-deck cars to run on that line, because the track was constructed using bull-head rail and not grooved rail. The Company converted the cars to single-deck and were left with six spare direct staircases.

Tramcar number 24 is being given its first test run on the Kidderminster system, with depot maintenance crew on the car. The gentleman standing on the step appears to be Mr A. Stewart, Traffic Superintendent.

NUMBER 29

Number 29 is a complete puzzle. Neither Stan Webb in his two volume "Black Country Tramways" or R. J. S. Wiseman in his updating of W. H. Bett and J. C. Gillham work "The Tramways of the West Midlands" have any reference to a tramcar with the fleet number 29. However, a commercial postcard of number 29 has come to light, photographed in Stourport, Bridge Street. Examination of the details of the car shows that the photograph was probably taken around 1901/1902. Its condition appears very new and it has a coupling for trailer operation (this finished around 1902). It also has an early design mesh life-tray and there are fittings for an oil lamp on the dash panel (replaced later by electric lamps on the batch of cars that included this car). The absence of any further photographs leads to speculation that when the batch was built by the Electric Railway and Tramway Carriage Works Ltd. in 1901 and delivered, this car was directed to Kidderminster for trials on the tramway. Presumably these did not go as well as hoped (some of the batch had their motors rewound to increase the top speed of the cars) and the car was returned to the Dudley and Stourbridge tramway, hence reducing the likelihood of the car being photographed in Kidderminster. The tramcars had removable oil headlights, seating for 22 inside the saloon and 26 on the upper deck with the original livery being orange and cream. The length of the saloon was 16ft 6ins, the overall length 27ft 6ins, with a 6ft wheelbase, an overall width of 6ft 5ins and a wheel diameter of 30ins.

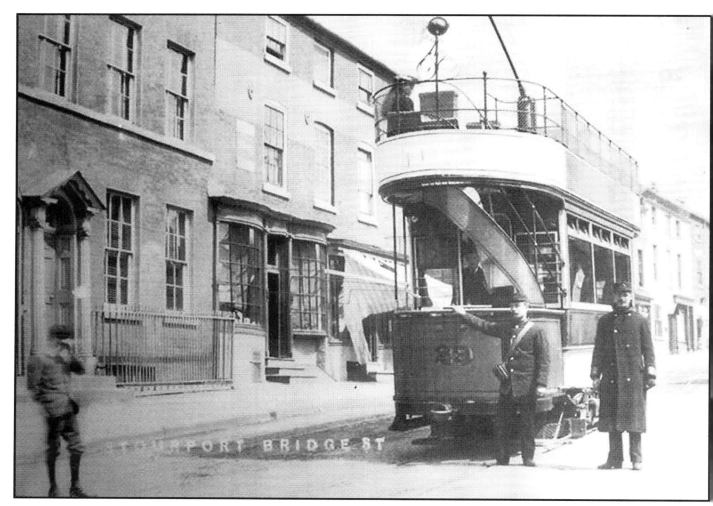

'Mystery' car number 29, standing at the Bridge Street terminus in Stourport.

NUMBER 11(2)

This car was a single-deck open-sided, crossbench motor car appearing in the fleet in 1903. Its origins are obscure and it is possible that it was the original trailer number 11 that was rebuilt and given motors in the way that numbers 7 – 9 had been. However, there is no confirmation of this speculation and the photographs of the car show distinct differences between this car and the original trailers.

Above: Tramcar number 11(2) waiting for a passing car at the Burlish loop. The presence of two conductors identifies the day as a Bank Holiday, while the driver is Francis Thompson, grandfather of Melvin Thompson, with whom I collaborated on the booklet "The Illustrated History of Kidderminster and Stourport Tramways". The two conductors were Alan Arley and William Harris.

Left: Tramcar number 15 was eleven years old when it was purchased by the Kidderminster system. Surprisingly it looks quite well for its age, but does illustrate that the system was the 'poor relation' in the BET group.

NUMBERS 15, 4(2), 10(3)

Number 15 was purchased in 1915 from the Birmingham District Company, having been built by Brush in 1904. It was an open-top double-deck car with direct stairs and a four-wheel Brill 21E truck. It appears to have retained its BDC fleet number. Two further similar cars were purchased second-hand around 1919 to replace cars 4 and 10, whose numbers they took. Later they were fitted with rudimentary windscreens to give the drivers some protection against adverse weather.

NUMBER 24(2)

This was a double-deck, open-top, four-wheel car with three side windows that joined the fleet in 1919. It was second-hand from Dudley and Stourbridge, having become redundant after they had acquired the new 'Tividale' type single-deck cars. It was built by the Electric Railway and Tramway Carriage Works in 1901 for the D&S to the standard Preston design with reversed stairs, these were later replaced with direct stairs before being transferred to Kidderminster. It seated 22 in the saloon and 27 on the upper deck. The saloon was 16ft 6ins long while the overall length was 27ft 6ins, the width was 6ft 5ins, on a 6ft wheelbase truck. Soon after arriving at Kidderminster it was fitted with full vestibules. No photographs have been found of this car.

NUMBER 3(2)

Number 3 was a single-deck, five-window saloon, four-wheel motor car. It was built by the Electric Railway and Tramway Carriage Works for the Kinver Light Railway in 1900. Three such cars were delivered and numbered 1 – 3. When the D&S took over the Kinver line they were renumbered to 43 – 45. The saloon length was 18ft 2ins, with an overall length over fenders of 27ft 2ins. They were 6ft 2ins wide and had 6ft 6ins wheelbase 'Lord Baltimore' trucks. In 1919 car number 43 was transferred to Kidderminster to replace its car number 3, which was the number the replacement was given. It was fitted with roof advertising boards (probably the ones from the original number 3). No photographs have been found of this car.

Tramcar number 2(2) at the Somerleyton terminus. This and car number 1(2) were around 15 years old when purchased by Kidderminster to replace the original 23 year old cars whose numbers they took.

NUMBERS 1(2) AND 2(2)

These were more second-hand cars from other B.E.T. systems. They were originally part of a larger batch built in 1904/5 by Brush for the Birmingham & Midland and City of Birmingham Companies. Built as double-deck, open-top, four-window cars, just prior to moving to Kidderminster, these two were rebuilt as single-deck cars with Brill 21E trucks and vestibules to protect the driver. They were to replace cars 1 and 2 in the Kidderminster fleet. Advertising boards (from cars 1 and 2) were fitted to the roof. They were also fitted with permanent destination boards reading "STATION AND SOMERLEYTON", indicating the role of these tramcars in the fleet.

Following the end of public service on the tramway (other than the statutory morning and evening workmen's cars) two Tividale type cars, numbers 4(₃) and 6(₂), were parked on a passing loop along Minster Road.

NUMBERS 71 [later renumbered 6(₂)], 2(₃), 4(₃) and 10(₄)

The history of these cars is as complex as the other cars in the fleet. They all came from a large number of the 'Tividale' design, all bar 10 were built in the Tividale Works (the other 10 coming from the Brush factory) in 1919-20. The Tividale design was revolutionary at the time. A totally-enclosed, single-deck, four-wheel car that was built without bulkheads, making the saloon feel very open. Two of this type of tramcar have been restored and now run at the Black Country Living Museum. They had 8ft 6ins Brill 21E trucks with 33ins diameter wheels. The bodies had an overall length of 33ft 2¼ins, were 6ft 6ins wide and 10ft 2ins high over the trolley plank. Number 71 was delivered new in 1919 and it was later renumbered 6 when the original car with that number was scrapped. Cars 2, 4 and 10 were delivered in the 1920s (probably between 1924 and 1926. They were all delivered in their Birmingham and Midland Tramways Joint Committee livery of Corinthian Green and cream.

LIVERY

1898 – 1929

Cars numbers 1 – 13, 19 and 25 had a livery officially described as orange-yellow and grey-white (also described as bright mustard yellow and pale cream or ivory). This was also the early livery on the other BET Black Country systems on the Dudley and Stourbridge; Kinver; and Dudley and Wolverhampton. The vestibule window sashes were brown; the roofs grey; and the trucks and solebars red oxide. The couplers were black and there was red, green and gold lining. The seats on the cross-bench cars were varnished wood.

1902 – 1912

Evidence is lacking but it seems that the enclosed single deck cars were repainted in a Munich Lake (also said to be crimson) and cream livery around 1902.

1909 – 1929

Again there is a lack of evidence for the exact change in livery to Corinthian Green (bright olive) and cream (ivory). The other BET systems that were part of the Birmingham and Midland Tramways Joint Committee changed to the Corinthian Green around 1909, however, Kidderminster did not join the Committee until 1915. With the limited facilities for large repairs and reconstruction of tramcars at Kidderminster, trams were sent to the Tividale works in the Black Country. It is likely that they were using the green paint and any repainted cars would have been given the green livery from 1909. But this is conjecture.

1918 – 1919

During the First World War paint supplies were restricted and the Company colours were no longer available. Repaired tramcars were given a coat of the only available paints, grey and white.

What Comberton Hill looked like on a Bank Holiday. Standing on the loop outside the station (the building behind the second and third cars is "The Railway Bell Hotel") are trams waiting for the day trippers going to Stourport. It was the substantial business from holiday makers that kept the tramway going. Behind car 19 is one of the original trailers, now motorised, the third car is number 11($_2$) and the fourth is another original trailer, now motorised

TECHNICAL SPECIFICATIONS

Recognising the British part of its name, the BET wished to demonstrate in the construction of its tramway that it sourced all the necessary equipment and components from British manufacturers. It particularly criticised those tramway promoters who used American products in the building of their tramways.

TRACK

The track was laid to what was the common gauge in the West Midlands, 3ft 6 ins, using girder rail of 75lb per yard. Throughout the 4½ mile long route it was single track with passing loops. In Kidderminster and Stourport the track was laid on a 6 ins thick base of concrete set between the rails and for 18 ins each side. The road surface was made of Clee Hill granite setts each 3 ins by 5 ins. The tramroad track, on a reserved way between the towns, was laid with transverse creosoted sleepers, the space between the rails and either side was made up with macadam (a road surface made of compressed layers of small broken stones). The rail joints were fixed with fishplates and bonded with copper wire.

The largest power station in the country was built at Stourport as part of the BET Group and opened in 1927, while the tramway last ran in 1929 and never saw the benefits of the new power plant.

A view along the High Street, Stourport showing the tramway track, but no tramcars. Today it would be foolish to stop in the middle of the road to have a chat.

HIGH STREET, STOURPORT.

OVERHEAD

The overhead was constructed using the Dickinson side trolley system, where the trolley wire could be as much as 11 feet from the centre of the car. The trolley wire was made of 0 BWG copper wire. Although the system was mainly single track, the overhead was a double wire throughout, obviating the need for frogs and reducing the size of the feeder cables. The traction poles were 6ins or 7ins diameter and 28ft long, planted 6ft in the ground and placed at an average of 150ft intervals. The trolley wire was the legally required 21ft above the road. The trolley wire was held on bracket arms, the longest being 8ft 6in, all manufactured by James Russell and Sons of Crown Tube Works, Wednesbury.

TRAMWAY POWER STATION

The power station was fitted with two Babcock and Wilcox boilers and a Greens economiser. Two Raworth 'Universal' steam engines of 200 hp were connected to dynamos (generators) made by the Brush Electrical Engineering Company. The electricity was produced by two six pole type generators that produced 550 volts at 190 amps (with a maximum load of 250 amps). There was a large switchboard with quick acting cut-out switches for overload conditions and a lightening arrester.

From the power station there were two feeder cables, one going towards the Comberton direction the other towards Stourport, each was buried 18ins under the ground. The former went half mile with a feeder box by the power station and one at the end of the feeder cable. At each feeder box the overhead wires were divided by section insulators. The box contained two knife switches, each with two cut-out fuses, so the box fed each of the double wires in both directions. This enabled any section of either wire to be isolated. In the other direction the feeder wire travelled 1½ miles to a feeder box, a further three boxes were located at half mile intervals, all being fitted as previously described. Finally, cables were laid connecting the rails of each terminus with the power station. This was to allow the measurement of the voltage drop over the tramway. It was a Board of Trade regulation that this should not exceed 7 volts.

ACKNOWLEDGEMENTS AND SOURCES

As previously noted, my first involvement with the history of the Kidderminster and Stourport tramway came in 1998 when I joined a group planning celebrations to recognise the centenary of the opening of the tramway. One of the projects was an illustrated pocket history of the line, that Melvyn Thompson and I wrote and published. Since then it has been in my mind to write a more comprehensive history of the line. I hesitated because there was already a detailed history forming part of Volume 2 of "Tramways of the Black Country" by Stan Webb. However, I continued to research the history and realised that Stan had focussed his history on the technical aspects of the line. There was a very full story of the social impact and effect on the townspeople that Stan had omitted. I thought I would see what impact the tramway had on the people of the two towns.

I spent time reading through the contemporaneous local newspapers, mainly the Kidderminster Shuttle. The notes of the various Council meetings were most enlightening, particularly on the relationships between the Councils and the tramway Company. Having completed that research I was then able to compare my findings with those detailed by Stan Webb in his books.

ACKNOWLEDGEMENTS

I would like to thank the staff of Kidderminster library and Worcester library, the Hive, who guided me in the right direction for material for the book.

I am indebted to Mike Ballinger for copies of correspondence between the Board of Trade and the tramway Company. As always my most grateful thanks go to Adam Gordon for once again agreeing to publish yet another of my books and Trevor Preece for applying his magic touch.

SOURCES

Berrows Worcester Journal 1896 – 1914
Kidderminster Shuttle, 1896 – 1930
Correspondence between the Board of Trade and the Tramway Company 1897—1912
Worcestershire Chronicle 1899 – 1901
Railway World, 2nd June 1898
The Electrical Engineer, 20th May 1898
The Engineer, 24th June 1898
Borough of Kidderminster Rules and Regulations made by the Mayor and Burgesses with Respect to the Tramways in the said Borough, 1899.
The Kidderminster & Stourport Electric Tramway Company, rules & regulations for officers and servants as from 16th March 1899, 58pp, reprinted by Adam Gordon, 1991.
Ordnance Survey map Stourport 1901
Kidderminster and Stourport Electric Tramway Company, booklet about visiting Stourport, published Kidderminster & Stourport Electric Tramway Company, c1901.
Kidderminster & District Electric Lighting and Traction Co. Ltd. British Electric Traction Co. Gazette volume 4, no.38, January 1902.
Stourport – The Popular Riverside Resort of the Midlands, published Kidderminster & Stourport Electric Tramway Company, 1906.
Ordnance Survey map Kidderminster 1921
Tramways of the Black Country by Stan Webb, published by the Author,1954.
Tramways of the Black Country, Volumes 1 and 2 by Stan Webb, published by the author 1974 and 1976.
The Illustrated History of Kidderminster and Stourport Electric Tramway Company by Melvyn Thompson and David Voice, published by David Voice Associates, 1998.
Kidderminster and Stourport Electric Tramway Company by Stephen Bragginton, Bob Milward, published online by Kidderminster Civic Society (Building Record 041), 2006.
Public Tramway Shelter, Oxford Street by Bob Milward, published online by Kidderminster Civic Society (Building Record 435), 2016.